MAJOR BENEFICIARIES OF THE IRAN DEAL: IRGC AND HEZBOLLAH

HEARING

BEFORE THE

SUBCOMMITTEE ON
THE MIDDLE EAST AND NORTH AFRICA

OF THE

COMMITTEE ON FOREIGN AFFAIRS
HOUSE OF REPRESENTATIVES

ONE HUNDRED FOURTEENTH CONGRESS

FIRST SESSION

SEPTEMBER 17, 2015

Serial No. 114–92

Printed for the use of the Committee on Foreign Affairs

Available via the World Wide Web: http://www.foreignaffairs.house.gov/ or
http://www.gpo.gov/fdsys/

U.S. GOVERNMENT PUBLISHING OFFICE

96–147PDF WASHINGTON : 2015

For sale by the Superintendent of Documents, U.S. Government Publishing Office
Internet: bookstore.gpo.gov Phone: toll free (866) 512–1800; DC area (202) 512–1800
Fax: (202) 512–2104 Mail: Stop IDCC, Washington, DC 20402–0001

COMMITTEE ON FOREIGN AFFAIRS

EDWARD R. ROYCE, California, *Chairman*

CHRISTOPHER H. SMITH, New Jersey
ILEANA ROS-LEHTINEN, Florida
DANA ROHRABACHER, California
STEVE CHABOT, Ohio
JOE WILSON, South Carolina
MICHAEL T. McCAUL, Texas
TED POE, Texas
MATT SALMON, Arizona
DARRELL E. ISSA, California
TOM MARINO, Pennsylvania
JEFF DUNCAN, South Carolina
MO BROOKS, Alabama
PAUL COOK, California
RANDY K. WEBER SR., Texas
SCOTT PERRY, Pennsylvania
RON DeSANTIS, Florida
MARK MEADOWS, North Carolina
TED S. YOHO, Florida
CURT CLAWSON, Florida
SCOTT DesJARLAIS, Tennessee
REID J. RIBBLE, Wisconsin
DAVID A. TROTT, Michigan
LEE M. ZELDIN, New York
DANIEL DONOVAN, New York

ELIOT L. ENGEL, New York
BRAD SHERMAN, California
GREGORY W. MEEKS, New York
ALBIO SIRES, New Jersey
GERALD E. CONNOLLY, Virginia
THEODORE E. DEUTCH, Florida
BRIAN HIGGINS, New York
KAREN BASS, California
WILLIAM KEATING, Massachusetts
DAVID CICILLINE, Rhode Island
ALAN GRAYSON, Florida
AMI BERA, California
ALAN S. LOWENTHAL, California
GRACE MENG, New York
LOIS FRANKEL, Florida
TULSI GABBARD, Hawaii
JOAQUIN CASTRO, Texas
ROBIN L. KELLY, Illinois
BRENDAN F. BOYLE, Pennsylvania

AMY PORTER, *Chief of Staff*   THOMAS SHEEHY, *Staff Director*
JASON STEINBAUM, *Democratic Staff Director*

————

SUBCOMMITTEE ON THE MIDDLE EAST AND NORTH AFRICA

ILEANA ROS-LEHTINEN, Florida, *Chairman*

STEVE CHABOT, Ohio
JOE WILSON, South Carolina
DARRELL E. ISSA, California
RANDY K. WEBER SR., Texas
RON DeSANTIS, Florida
MARK MEADOWS, North Carolina
TED S. YOHO, Florida
CURT CLAWSON, Florida
DAVID A. TROTT, Michigan
LEE M. ZELDIN, New York

THEODORE E. DEUTCH, Florida
GERALD E. CONNOLLY, Virginia
BRIAN HIGGINS, New York
DAVID CICILLINE, Rhode Island
ALAN GRAYSON, Florida
GRACE MENG, New York
LOIS FRANKEL, Florida
BRENDAN F. BOYLE, Pennsylvania

CONTENTS

MAJOR BENEFICIARIES OF THE IRAN DEAL: IRGC AND HEZBOLLAH

THURSDAY, SEPTEMBER 17, 2015

House of Representatives,
Subcommittee on the Middle East and North Africa,
Committee on Foreign Affairs,
Washington, DC.

The subcommittee met, pursuant to notice, at 2:07 p.m., in room 2172, Rayburn House Office Building, Hon. Ileana Ros-Lehtinen (chairman of the subcommittee) presiding.

Ms. ROS-LEHTINEN. The subcommittee will come to order.

After recognizing myself and Ranking Member Deutch for 5 minutes each for our opening statements, I will then recognize any other member seeking recognition for a minute. We will then hear from our witnesses.

And, without objection, your prepared statements, madam and gentlemen, your prepared statements will be made part of the record.

Members may have 5 days to insert statements and questions for the record, subject to the length limitation of the rules.

The Chair now recognizes herself for her remarks.

As we confront the fallout from the Iran nuclear deal, it is important that we examine two critical networks, as they are two critical criminal networks—that stand to gain the most from sanctions relief: The Islamic Revolutionary Guard Corps and Iran's proxy, Hezbollah.

Made up of at least 150,000 personnel, the Revolutionary Guard Corps is responsible for Iran's external and internal security, including the protection of the key strategic oil waterway, the Strait of Hormuz; the development of Iran's ballistic missile program; and maintaining order and control of the Iranian people.

It oversees the Quds Force, the asymmetric war and terror operators of the IRGC, who are behind the deaths of hundreds of American service men and women and coalition forces in Iraq and who continue to plan operations on the ground in Iraq and Syria while undermining our national security interests.

The IRGC is Iran's single largest economic actor. It owns the country's largest construction company, its main telecommunications company, and controls at least 25 percent of the Tehran Stock Exchange. The IRGC owns and controls banks, its officials sit on and control the boards of private companies, and it is the primary player in the construction and infrastructure sectors as well as, increasingly, the energy sector.

(1)

Because the IRGC controls so much of the Iranian economy, it is poised to gain billions from the deal and Iran's economic growth. When the administration argues that the Iranian regime will invest its sanctions relief into infrastructure, what they are not telling you is that the IRGC, a terror organization in its own right, will be the one cashing in on all the infrastructure, all the construction, all the energy projects. Companies are already lining up to do business with Iran, and, as the sanctions come off, more money will be funneled to IRGC companies, who will then turn right around and use that money for their nefarious activities.

As such a big player in Iran, the IRGC has a vested interest in maintaining its alliance with the regime and ensuring the regime's survival, both inside Iran by maintaining its authority over the people of Iran but also by continuing to expand regionally and fulfilling its hegemonic ambitions.

Fulfilling those ambitions requires the continued work of the Quds Force—training Shia militias in Iraq, funneling funds and arms to Syria's Bashar al-Assad, and supporting Houthi fighters in Yemen. Incredibly, the Iran deal delists and lifts certain sanctions from some of the same people leading these very actions, including the current Quds Force commander, Soleimani, and the former Quds Force commander and Defense Minister Vahidi. And, as we know, he is wanted by Interpol for his role in the AMIA Jewish community center bombings in Buenos Aires.

As a matter of fact, almost half of the entire nuclear agreement is pages and pages of delisting of individuals, of companies, and vessels from the U.S. or EU sanctions list.

The second organization that will benefit enormously from sanctions relief is one of the world's most dangerous and capable terror organizations, Hezbollah. Trained, equipped, and funded by the Quds Force, Hezbollah is said to be responsible for some of the world's most infamous terror attacks, including the 1983 U.S. Marine barracks bombing in Beirut, the AMIA Jewish community center which I just referenced, and the 1996 Khobar Towers bombing, just to name a few.

A stronger Hezbollah undermines our interests in Lebanon, where that fragile country continues to grapple with internal strife. And its forces are deeply involved and critically important to Iranian efforts in Syria, helping Iran to prop up Assad and prolonging the chaos, the destruction, the tragedy that is spreading further and further outside the borders of Syria.

Hezbollah's leader recently reaffirmed the terror organization's ideological partnership with Iran, saying that the nuclear deal would not stop Iran from providing it material and financial support. And now that we have lifted Iran's arms embargo and ballistic missile sanctions, Hezbollah will soon be able to obtain even more sophisticated weaponry in order to carry out operations like the one we recently saw with a terror cell in Kuwait.

Sanctions relief from the Iranian deal will not only free up resources for Iran to spend more on Assad, it will allow Hezbollah to extricate itself from Syria, where its forces have been bogged down, and return to its focus of its top priority and target: The democratic Jewish State of Israel. The possibility that Hezbollah will launch attacks against Israel is increasingly likely thanks to the Iran deal and Iran's increasing capability to provide assistance and advanced weaponry.

We must consider the impact of both direct and indirect sanctions relief from the Iran deal and what these additional resources will do for the Iranian regime's next steps in the region, including what it will do for the capabilities of Iran's proxies, like Hezbollah, and the consequences for our own interests and the interests of our allies.

I look forward to hearing from our witnesses on exactly who and which entities stand to gain the most from this disastrous agreement, what we can expect next from the IRGC and Hezbollah, and what we here in Congress can do to prevent this from happening.

So pleased to yield to the ranking member, Mr. Deutch of Florida.

Mr. DEUTCH. Thank you, Madam Chairman.

And while this is not the first hearing we have had to look at Iran's sponsorship of terrorism, it takes on new significance in the wake of the nuclear agreement, as Iran stands to gain access to billions of dollars.

After the Iran deal debate, it is important that the administration and my colleagues continue to be clear about the nature of this regime. Iran was designated a state sponsor of terror in January 1984, after it orchestrated the deadly U.S. Embassy bombing in Beirut which killed 63, the horrific attack on the Marine barracks that killed 241 U.S. servicemembers, and the bombings of the U.S. and French Embassies in Kuwait. Both 1983 attacks were carried out by what would become Hezbollah.

Despite the U.S. designation in 1984, in September of that year Hezbollah carried out another attack on the U.S. Embassy annex in Beirut, killing 23. It was Hezbollah that hijacked TWA Flight 847, resulting in the death of a U.S. Navy diver. It was Hezbollah that bombed the Israeli Embassy in Argentina and the AMIA Jewish center in the early 1990s.

It was a Hezbollah-linked group that bombed the Khobar Towers in Saudi Arabia, killing 19 U.S. Air Force personnel in 1996. It was Hezbollah that blew up a tourist bus of Israelis in Bulgaria in 2012. And it was Hezbollah that attempted to carry out dozens of foiled terrorist attacks around the world—all of this done, of course, with financial and material support from, and at the direction of, the Iranian regime.

Iran has continued to supply Hezbollah with weaponry to fight alongside Assad's forces in Syria. Weapons transfers from Iran to Hezbollah have allowed the terrorist organization to amass an arsenal of nearly 100,000 rockets in Lebanon, with the ability to reach every corner of Israel. Iran's terror proxies are directed by the Iranian Revolutionary Guard Corps' elite Quds Force, led by the infamous general Qasem Soleimani, who has been spotted on the battlefields of Iraq and, according to reports, may have just recently again visited Russia, his partner in Syria. The IRGC is aiding the Houthis in Yemen and stirring unrest via their allies in countries throughout the Gulf.

The IRGC is the most powerful economic actor in Iran. In fact, no one has benefited under sanctions more than the potentially hundreds of IRGC-owned companies that no longer had to deal with international competition for construction or energy projects, and no one will likely benefit more when these IRGC-owned companies are delisted and sector-based sanctions removed.

Now, there are certainly disagreements over exactly what Iran will do with its sanctions relief. No doubt this regime, which is obsessed with its own survival, will use money to revitalize Iran's economy. President Hassan Rouhani was elected on his pledges to bring real economic relief to the people of Iran, and, by all accounts, he wants to deliver. But it is logical that some portion of Iran's newfound wealth will flow to its terror proxies. And regardless of how you feel about the nuclear deal, no one can dispute that Iran remains the world's largest state sponsor of terrorism.

Despite crushing U.S. international sanctions, Iran has sustained its destabilizing activity with relatively limited resources, but that will soon change. In fact, not only did Iran receive sanctions relief, but it received repeal of the arms embargo and ban on the transfer of ballistic missile technologies in 5 and 8 years respectively. Now we are faced with the reality of advanced weaponry sales to Iran that will undoubtedly fall into the hands of Hezbollah, Hamas, Shiite militias, and other bad actors like Al Shabaab in East Africa.

The IRGC already possesses ballistic missile capabilities that threaten its neighbors. Now, in 8 years, it will be free to purchase technologies to advance its program. This committee held a hearing on Iran's quest for intercontinental ballistic missiles earlier this summer, where experts testified that the only logical use for an ICBM is the delivery of a nuclear warhead.

My colleagues on this committee are split on support for the JCPOA, but we cannot allow our already-expressed positions to hinder our efforts to work together to do whatever we can to block Iran's ability to exploit its anticipated windfall for dangerous and destructive activities.

We must now come together for a practical discussion on what more the United States can do to counter Iran's destabilizing activities in the region and around the world. This means increasing intelligence cooperation with Gulf partners, strengthening the capabilities of our friends in the region, enhancing Israel's qualitative military edge, redoubling our efforts to interdict weapons shipments, and continuing to enforce existing and to impose new sanctions against those who support terrorism or engage in human rights abuses. If they received nuclear proliferation sanctions relief under the deal but they support terror or abuse human rights, then the individuals or entities must continue to be sanctioned.

I look forward to hearing from our experts today as to what steps the U.S. and the international community can take to blunt the impact of Iran's newfound financial resources and the strengthening of the dangerous regime.

And I yield back.

Ms. ROS-LEHTINEN. Thank you very much, Mr. Deutch.

Mr. Cicilline.

Mr. CICILLINE. Thank you, Madam Chairman and Ranking Member Deutch, for calling this hearing today.

It is absolutely critical that, as the Joint Comprehensive Plan of Action is implemented, Congress and the administration are relentless and vigilant in monitoring its implementation and that we work together with Israel and with our allies in Europe and the Middle East to combat the destabilizing activity of Iran throughout the region.

In order to strengthen its implementation, Congress should introduce legislation as necessary, and I look forward to working with my colleagues on this committee in doing so to ensure that the necessary steps are taken.

In particular, I have expressed to the President my strong support for an expedited renewal of the Israeli defense agreement for a new 10-year period. And, of course, robust funding must be provided by Congress. Additionally, Congress must provide additional financial resources to support the implementation and monitoring process through the IAEA and increase funding for U.S. intelligence and diplomatic activities.

The administration must also develop a specific plan with the P5+1 and Israel to respond to any violations of the Joint Comprehensive Plan of Action by Iran and to work together to confront Iran's destabilizing activities in the region. In addition, we must continue to aggressively pursue appropriate non-nuclear sanctions against individuals and organizations responsible for terrorism activity and violations of human rights.

There is no question that the IRGC and Hezbollah will continue to take actions to support terrorism throughout the region, and it is incumbent upon the United States to ensure that we have a robust action plan to combat these activities in close cooperation with our allies. I look forward to hearing the witnesses' suggestions for actions we can take to mitigate the dangers posed by Hezbollah and the IRGC.

And I thank the witnesses for being here.

And, with that, I yield back.

Ms. Ros-Lehtinen. Thank you very much, Mr. Cicilline.

Ms. Meng of New York.

Ms. Meng. Thank you, Chairwoman Ros-Lehtinen and Ranking Member Deutch, for your longstanding stellar leadership here. I know that you have worked closely and very hard on issues of terrorism, Iran's funding of it, and this recent deal very closely.

While I appreciate that many of my colleagues have voiced disapproval of the Joint Comprehensive Plan of Action during last week's vote, I am troubled with the prospect of it moving forward. In addition to the direct outcome of the Iran deal with regards to nuclear capabilities, there are serious concerns about Iran's access to funds, especially given their track record of funding universally recognized terrorist groups.

I am interested in hearing the consequences of this deal as it relates to these beneficiaries and ways that we can mitigate any potentially disastrous outcomes.

Thank you. I yield back.

Ms. Ros-Lehtinen. Thank you so much.

And hearing no other requests for time, I am pleased to present our panel.

First, we are pleased to welcome Dr. Emanuele Ottolenghi, who is a senior fellow at the Foundation for Defense of Democracies. Previously, Dr. Emanuele headed the Transatlantic Institute in

Brussels, and he has advised several foreign ministries in Europe on the subject of Iran.

We welcome you, sir.

Second, we welcome back a good friend of our subcommittee, Dr. Matthew Levitt, director of the Stein Program on Counterterrorism and Intelligence for the Washington Institute for Near East Policy. Previously, Dr. Levitt served as the Deputy Assistant Secretary of Intelligence and Analysis at the U.S. Department of the Treasury, a branch chief under the Director of National Intelligence, and a counterterrorism advisor to the State Department's Special Envoy to the Middle East.

Welcome back.

And last but certainly not least, we welcome back Dr. Suzanne Maloney, who is the interim deputy director of the foreign policy program for the Brookings Institution. Dr. Maloney has served as an external advisor to the State Department on issues related to Iran. She has also served as a policy planner for the Middle East for the Secretary of State and the director of the Council on Foreign Relations' task force on U.S. policy toward Iran.

Welcome to all three. Your written remarks will be made a part of the record. Please feel free to summarize.

And we will begin with you, Dr. Emanuele.

STATEMENT OF EMANUELE OTTOLENGHI, PH.D., SENIOR FELLOW, FOUNDATION FOR DEFENSE OF DEMOCRACIES

Mr. OTTOLENGHI. Thank you, Chairman Ros-Lehtinen, Ranking Member Deutch, and members of the committee. On behalf of FDD and its Center on Sanctions and Illicit Finance, I am very grateful for the opportunity to testify.

Iran's Islamic Revolutionary Guard is the regime's top exporter of terrorism and a deadly instrument of domestic repression. My testimony describes how, regrettably, the Guards will benefit greatly from the Joint Comprehensive Plan of Action.

The JCPOA dismantles most of the international nuclear sanctions against Iran, thereby creating a major stimulus package for its economy. The IRGC and the Supreme Leader's business empire will be its main beneficiaries. Their economic ascendance will fortify their domestic influence.

Although the U.S. retains the legal edifice of sanctions against the IRGC, it is insufficient to exclude the IRGC from this windfall for four reasons: First, on implementation day, just months from now, the JCPOA lifts or suspends sanctions against entire sectors of the Iranian economy. The IRGC is active in each sector. IRGC companies will get the lion's share of business opportunities.

Second, the lifting of sectoral bans will provide the IRGC easier access to dual-use technology in the aerospace, defense, and nuclear sectors.

Third, on implementation day, the JCPOA will delist companies that assisted the IRGC's nuclear and missile procurement efforts, as well as its support for Hamas and Hezbollah and for the Assad regime in Syria. A change of behavior was not a condition for their delisting.

Fourth, most IRGC companies were never identified as such by EU or U.S. authorities. Treasury has listed only 19 IRGC individuals, 23 companies, 4r military entities, and 2 academic institutions. The EU has listed just 25 companies. My written testimony names hundreds of companies owned or controlled by the IRGC that should have been designated.

Absent the change in approach by Congress or the administration, the post-sanctions economic climate will likely benefit the IRGC because, in practice, the global business community looks to the U.S. Treasury for a way to assess risk. Companies seeking to reenter Iran will assume that what is not explicitly forbidden is allowed.

Let me offer you the example of Iran Aluminum Company, or IRALCO, Iran's largest aluminum producer. The EU sanctioned it in 2012 because it had assisted Iran's nuclear procurement, including a contract to supply aluminum to Iran's Centrifuge Technology Company. The U.S. never designated IRALCO, even though it is partially owned by an IRGC investment company that is under U.S. sanctions. And because IRALCO was only sanctioned for nuclear-related activities, the EU will delist it on implementation day.

Madam Chairman, I therefore strongly recommend that, first, there be an increase in U.S. designations against the IRGC because of the IRGC's unequivocal role in terrorism and other nefarious activities. If Congress and Treasury were to designate hundreds of IRGC companies before implementation day, this would send a very strong message to the business community contemplating Iranian contracts.

Second, to help this process along, Congress should require Treasury to lower the threshold for designations. As I explain in greater detail in my written testimony, the IRGC has engaged in a pattern of obfuscation to hide its control of many corporations. Even with a minority share, the IRGC often controls these companies through the board of directors. Congress can also mandate that Treasury maintain and publish an IRGC watchlist to identify and report on companies that do not yet reach the designation threshold.

Third, Congress should also require the State Department to designate the IRGC as a foreign terrorist organization. Designating the IRGC as an FTO will provide another warning to foreign companies considering business in Iran. Listing the IRGC as an FTO will also emphasize that the IRGC cannot be decoupled from the Quds Force; they are one and the same.

Fourth, Congress can leverage future trade agreements with Europe to limit the IRGC's operations there. Congress should require the Transatlantic Trade and Investment Partnership between the U.S. and the EU to stipulate that any European company contracting with Iran must certify that none of the business partners are associated in part or in whole with the IRGC, requiring also that the EU report annually on European companies investing in Iran, placing local merchant transactions under public scrutiny. At a minimum, Congress should encourage international corporations to demand an exclusion clause to halt commercial activities with all suspected or designated IRGC entities.

These are just a few highlights from my written testimony. I thank you for the opportunity to testify, and I very much look forward to your questions.

[The prepared statement of Mr. Ottolenghi follows:]

Congressional Testimony

The Iran Nuclear Deal and its Impact on Iran's Islamic Revolutionary Guards Corps

Dr. Emanuele Ottolenghi

Foundation for Defense of Democracies

Center on Sanctions and Illicit Finance

Hearing before the House Committee on Foreign Affairs

Middle East and North Africa Subcommittee

Washington, DC

September 17, 2015

FDD

FOUNDATION FOR
DEFENSE OF DEMOCRACIES

1726 M Street NW • Suite 700 • Washington, DC 20036

Chairman Ros-Lehtinen, Ranking Member Deutch, members of the committee, on behalf of the Foundation for Defense of Democracies and its Center on Sanctions and Illicit Finance, I thank you for the opportunity to testify.

This testimony will focus on the impact of the Joint Comprehensive Plan of Action (JCPOA) on Iran's Islamic Revolutionary Guard Corps (IRGC) and its dominant position in Iran's economy.

The IRGC is the custodian of Iran's best-kept military secrets, including its clandestine nuclear military program and ballistic missile program. As the regime's Praetorian Guard, it is also charged with defending the Islamic Revolution from enemies at home and spreading the revolution abroad. Over the years, the IRGC has zealously fulfilled these tasks, quashing pro-democracy protesters inside Iran and sponsoring terrorism and Islamist movements abroad.

The JCPOA dismantles specific United Nations and European Union sanctions, and significantly diminishes the scope and reach of U.S. sanctions.

In doing so, the JCPOA creates a major "stimulus package" for Iran's economy. The IRGC derives much of its domestic clout from its position of dominance within Iran's economy. Thus, the IRGC and the supreme leader's business empire will be the main beneficiaries. Their economic ascendance will fortify their domestic political influence.

As export and trade restrictions are lifted, previously prohibited Western technology will make its way back to Iran. The challenge of denying the IRGC access to banned technology – including dual-use technology and equipment for monitoring dissidents – will become even more arduous. The demise of sanctions will also facilitate the acquisition of advanced weaponry that will improve Tehran's conventional military capabilities, as well as its support for the Bashar al-Assad regime in Syria, Hamas in the Gaza Strip, Hezbollah in Lebanon, and Houthi rebels in Yemen.

To be clear, the United States is set to maintain its sanctions on the IRGC. The JCPOA does not alter them. Moreover, the European Union will not delist most IRGC entities on its sanctions list until Transition Day, roughly eight years from now. But as this testimony explains, once the bulk of Iran sanctions are lifted, the remaining measures against the IRGC are insufficient. They will not isolate the Guards and the supreme leader's business interests from the benefits that the JCPOA will generate.

First, on Implementation Day – likely several months from now – the JCPOA requires the European Union, United States, and United Nations to lift or suspend sanctions against entire sectors of the Iranian economy. The IRGC and the supreme leader's business interests are active in many sectors – some of which they dominate almost completely. IRGC companies will get the lion's share of public contracts and business opportunities.

Second, on Implementation Day, numerous companies will be delisted that have served as accessories to IRGC nuclear and ballistic missile programs, as well as support for the Assad regime and its crimes against humanity. This includes the entire network of companies and subsidiaries controlled by the supreme leader, as well as Iran's aviation industry and state-owned shipping firms, and companies where the IRGC has a significant ownership interest.

The delisting is not the result of a demonstrable change in these entities' patterns of behavior. Rather, they are being delisted because the JCPOA requires the wholesale lifting of sanctions on entire sectors. There are no guarantees these entities will, once delisted, cease the illicit conduct that caused them to be sanctioned in the first place – instead, there is ample reason to believe they will redouble that activity.

Third, companies owned or controlled by the IRGC that have until now eluded designation by the U.S., EU, or UN are now likely to benefit from the post-JCPOA windfall, as the business community will accept them as legitimate business partners. The same is true for IRGC senior executives that eluded sanctions until now.

Meanwhile, Tehran will challenge every attempt to impose new sanctions, as it did with designations announced by the U.S. Treasury following the November 2013 interim nuclear deal.[1] New sanctions will trigger an Iranian request for consultation with the United States, potentially followed by a referral to the Joint Commission's Working Group, as stipulated under section 7.3 of Annex IV of the JCPOA.[2] Tehran may also challenge new sanctions under Section 2.1.14. This clause states that the Joint Commission (of which Iran is a member) will review "any issue that a JCPOA participant believes constitutes nonperformance by another JCPOA participant."[3]

The IRGC and the Supreme Leader's Business Empires

Sanctions against the IRGC were a central component of the complex architecture of punitive and restrictive measures that the U.S., EU, and UN built over the course of the past decade. According to the U.S. Treasury:

> "The IRGC has a growing presence in Iran's financial and commercial sectors and extensive economic interests in the defense production, construction, and oil industries, controlling billions of dollars in corporate business...imposing financial sanctions on commercial enterprises of the IRGC has a direct impact on revenues that could be used by the IRGC to facilitate illicit conduct."[4]

---

[1] Fredrick Dahl & Adrian Croft, "Iran angry over U.S. sanctions, nuclear talks interrupted," *Reuters*, December 13, 2013. (http://www.reuters.com/article/2013/12/13/us-iran-nuclear-sanctions-idUSBRE9BC0CY20131213)
[2] "Joint Comprehensive Plan of Action, Annex IV – Joint Commission" Vienna, July 14, 2015. Section 7.3. (http://eeas.europa.eu/statements-eeas/docs/iran_agreement/annex_4_joint_commission_en.pdf)
[3] "Joint Comprehensive Plan of Action, Annex IV – Joint Commission" Vienna, July 14, 2015. Section 2.1.14. (http://eeas.europa.eu/statements-eeas/docs/iran_agreement/annex_4_joint_commission_en.pdf)
[4] U.S. Department of the Treasury, Press Release, "Fact Sheet: Treasury Sanctions Major Iranian Commercial Entities" June 4, 2013. (http://www.treasury.gov/press-center/press-releases/Pages/tg1217.aspx)

The JCPOA reverses that impact by directly and indirectly increasing revenues of the IRGC's commercial enterprises. The JCPOA also lifts sanctions against the "Headquarters for Executing the Order of the Imam" (EIKO), a vast holding company controlled by the supreme leader with assets and commercial operations worth an estimated $95 billion.[5] While EIKO is not formally part of the IRGC, it frequently partners with Guard companies. Like the Guard, it has an opaque, parallel quasi-state power structure.

On June 4, 2013, Treasury sanctioned EIKO and 37 of its subsidiaries[6] – including a number of foreign companies – under Executive Order 13599, which targeted Iran's government-owned entities for posing a threat to the integrity of the international financial system. As Treasury explained:

> "EIKO has made tens of billions of dollars in profit for the Iranian regime each year through the exploitation of favorable loan rates from Iranian banks and the sale and management of real estate holdings, including selling property donated to EIKO. EIKO has also confiscated properties in Iran that were owned by Iranians not living in Iran full-time... EIKO has been tasked with assisting the Iranian Government's circumvention of U.S. and international sanctions. Because of this unique mission, EIKO has received all of the funding it needs to facilitate transactions through its access to the Iranian leadership."[7]

U.S. sanctions had a chilling effect on EIKO's business ventures abroad, especially in Europe.[8] An EIKO subsidiary, Tadbir Energy Group, unsuccessfully bid for a refinery in France in 2012;[9] and in April 2015, another EIKO bid to buy a refinery in Switzerland was rejected, reportedly due to concerns over U.S. sanctions.[10]

With Washington set to delist all of EIKO's subsidiaries on Implementation Day,[11] barriers to conducting business with EIKO are already eroding. In January 2015, representatives of two

---

[5] Steven Stecklow, Babak Deghghanpisheh & Yeganeh Torbati, "Assets of the Ayatollah", *Reuters*, November 13, 2013. (http://www.reuters.com/investigates/iran/#article/part1)

[6] U.S. Department of Treasury, Resource Center, "Iran Designations," June 4, 2013. (http://www.treasury.gov/resource-center/sanctions/OFAC-Enforcement/Pages/20130604.aspx)

[7] U.S. Department of Treasury, Press Release. "Treasury Targets Assets of Iranian Leadership" June 4, 2013, (http://www.treasury.gov/press-center/press-releases/Pages/jl1968.aspx)

[8] Emanuele Ottolenghi & Saeed Ghasseminejad. "The Iranian Deep State is Trying to Buy an Oil Refinery in Switzerland Even Before Sanctions Have Been Lifted," *Business Insider*, April 29, 2015. (http://www.businessinsider.com/iranian-deep-state-trying-to-buy-swiss-oil-refinery-2015-4)

[9] Benoit Faucon, "Iran's Tadbir Energy to Bid for French Refinery," *The Wall Street Journal*, July 4, 2012. (http://www.wsj.com/articles/SB10001424052702303962304577507370495110742)

[10] Emanuele Ottolenghi & Saeed Ghasseminejad, "The Iranian Deep State is Trying to Buy an Oil Refinery in Switzerland Even Before Sanctions Have Been Lifted," *Business Insider*, April 29, 2015. (http://www.businessinsider.com/iranian-deep-state-trying-to-buy-swiss-oil-refinery-2015-4)

[11] See Emanuele Ottolenghi & Saeed Ghasseminejad, "Under Iran Agreement, U.S. Will Delist All Entities Controlled by Supreme Leader" *Foundation for Defense of Democracies*, July 27, 2015. (http://www.defenddemocracy.org/media-hit/ottolenghi-ghasseminejad-us-will-delist-entities-controlled-by-khamenei/); U.S. restrictions will remain in place against EIKO and its designated subsidiaries for U.S. persons as defined in the JCPOA. According to footnote 6 of Annex II of the JCPOA, "For the purposes of Sections 4 and 6-7

sanctioned EIKO petrochemical companies were in Moscow attending Interplastica, a large plastics and rubber trade fair.[12] In August, a subsidiary of Italy's Finmeccanica signed a $530-million contract with EIKO subsidiary Ghadir Investment to build an electric power plant in Iran. The deal was signed during an official visit to Tehran by Italy's Economic Development Minister Federica Guidi and Foreign Minister Paolo Gentiloni.[13] According to the U.S. Treasury, Ghadir is a subsidiary of EIKO.[14]

The delisting of EIKO will facilitate more such deals across Europe. It may also weaken the level of scrutiny that export-control authorities have paid to EIKO's subsidiaries.

The arrest of EIKO executive Behrouz Dolatzadeh is a case in point. Dolatzadeh was arrested in Prague in February 2012, and charged by Czech authorities with attempting to buy 3,500 U.S.-made M-4 assault rifles for Iran's military.[15] According to *Reuters*,[16] at the time of his arrest, Dolatzadeh was working for EIKO. He was convicted by a Czech court but then released, in September 2013, upon winning his appeal on a technicality even though Czech prosecutors appealed his release to the Czech Supreme Court.[17]

---

of this JCPOA, the term 'non-U.S. person' means any individual or entity, excluding (i) any United States citizen, permanent resident alien, entity organised under the laws of the United States or any jurisdiction within the United States (including foreign branches), or any person in the United States, and (ii) any entity owned or controlled by a U.S. person. For the purposes of (ii) of the preceding sentence, an entity is 'owned or controlled' by a U.S. person if the U.S. person: (i) holds a 50 percent or greater equity interest by vote or value in the entity; (ii) holds a majority of seats on the board of directors of the entity; or (iii) otherwise controls the actions, policies, or personnel decisions of the entity. U.S. persons and U.S.-owned or -controlled foreign entities will continue to be generally prohibited from conducting transactions of the type permitted pursuant to this JCPOA, unless authorised to do so by the U.S. Department of the Treasury's Office of Foreign Assets Control (OFAC)." "Joint Comprehensive Plan of Action, Annex II – Sanctions related commitments" Vienna, July 14, 2015. (http://eeas.europa.eu/statements-eeas/docs/iran_agreement/annex_2_sanctions_related_commitments_en.pdf)

[12] The two companies are Polynar Petrochemical Co. and Ghaed Bassir Petrochemical Products Co. "Powerful Presence of Iranian Petrochemical Companies at Interplastica 2015," *Interplastica*, accessed September 13, 2015. (http://www.interplastica.de/cipp/md_ww2/custom/pub/content.oid.32498/lang.2/ticket.g_u_e_s_t/~/Powerful_Presence_of_Iranian_Petrochemical_Companies_at_INTERPLASTICA_2015.html)

[13] "Iran-Italia: Ministro Guidi, Raggiungimento Intesa per Accordo fra Italiana Fata e Iraniana Ghadir per Centrale Elettrica Combinata" *Agenzia Nova*, August 9, 2015. (http://www.agenzianova.com/a/0/1191780/2015-08-09/business-news-ministro-guidi-intesa-fra-italiana-fata-e-iraniana-ghadir-per-centrale-elettrica-combinata)

[14] U.S. Department of Treasury, Press Release, "Treasury Targets Assets of Iranian Leadership" June 4, 2013, (http://www.treasury.gov/press-center/press-releases/Pages/jl1968.aspx)

[15] "Freight Forwarders Banned, Imprisoned and Fined for Illegal Logistics Operations," *Handy Shipping Guide*, March 1, 2012. (http://www.handyshippingguide.com/shipping-news/freight-forwarders-banned-imprisoned-and-fined-for-illegal-logistics-operations_3494)

[16] Steve Stecklow, "Exclusive: Iranian linked to Setad wanted by the U.S. for attempted arms smuggling," *Reuters*, December 18, 2013. (http://www.reuters.com/article/2013/12/18/us-setad-fugitive-idUSBRE9BH0D020131218)

[17] According to Reuters' Steve Stecklow, the Czech court of appeals determined that his conviction was the result of entrapment by U.S. and Czech authorities. See Steve Stecklow, "Exclusive: Iranian linked to Setad wanted by the U.S. for attempted arms smuggling," *Reuters*, December 18, 2013. (http://www.reuters.com/article/2013/12/18/us-setad-fugitive-idUSBRE9BH0D020131218)

Although a federal grand jury indicted him in Arizona in February 2012,[18] the U.S. did not request Dolatzadeh's extradition. Nor did Treasury designate the complex web of companies that Dolatzadeh established in Istanbul and in the Georgian cities of Tbilisi and Poti. Corporate entries show that once he was arrested, Dolatzadeh transferred ownership of these companies to another Iranian national, Jafar Kaviani, who is also an executive of a company owned by EIKO.[19] Treasury has taken no action on Kaviani, either.

Worryingly, companies EIKO likely established for the purpose of evading sanctions and helping Iranian procurement efforts will now be subject to even less scrutiny than before the JCPOA.

IRGC Sanctions Windfall on Major Economic Sectors

The JCPOA will lift blanket bans on commercial and financial transactions in entire sectors of Iran's economy. That step contains three elements: sanctioned companies will be delisted by both the EU and U.S.; the EU will allow economic activities with Iran; and U.S. secondary sanctions against these sectors will be removed, continuing only to affect U.S. persons as defined in the agreement.

The lifting of sanctions will further boost Tehran's economic recovery following the temporary easing of sanctions provided by the 2013 interim agreement. According to the World Bank:

> "The Iranian economy rebounded out of recession, with growth estimated at 3.0% in 2014 compared to a contraction of 1.7% in 2013. This comes as a result of the temporary and partial easing of sanctions imposed on Iran's oil exports, on the supply chain in key sectors of the economy—such as in the automobiles industry—and on the transactions of international and domestic banks, as well as a rise in consumer and business confidence."[20]

A recently released report issued by the Foundation for Defense of Democracies and Roubini Global Economics suggests that Iran's future economic growth might be even more vigorous:

> "An average growth of more than 4-5% in the three years starting [next year] is plausible if Iranian authorities continue economic reforms and begin to attract investment, and if Tehran is able to significantly boost oil exports."[21]

---

[18] *United States of America v. Dolatzadeh*, Indictment, 2:12-cr-00258-DGC (D. AZ., February 7 2012).
[19] In June 2013, Dolatzadeh transferred ownership of his shares at Turkish company's Blue Sky General Trading Bilgi Teknolojileri ic ve dis Ticaret Limited Sirketi to Kaviani, who according to the Tehran Chamber of Commerce, Industry and Mines entries (http://www.tccim.ir/dir/english/CompFullDetail.aspx?cid=49&id=35&pid=35), is managing director for Ofogh Afroz Ima (http://www.tejaratalmas.com/images/nl/holding/ofoghafroz.jpg), a company owned by EIKO's investing subsidiary Tejarat Almas Mobin (http://www.tejaratalmas.com/index.html#).
[20] World Bank, Countries, "Iran Country overview," accessed September 8, 2015. (http://www.worldbank.org/en/country/iran/overview)
[21] Mark Dubowitz, Annie Fixler, & Rachel Ziemba, "Iran's Mysterious Shrinking Reserves: Estimating the Value of Tehran's Foreign Assets" *Foundation for Defense of Democracies & Roubini Global Economics*, September 2015.

The IRGC investment portfolio is robust, including substantial shares in 14 companies publicly traded on Tehran's Stock Exchange (TSE) with a combined value of $17 billion. There are an additional 13 publicly traded companies with significant ownership by the IRGC, Armed Forces, and Basij. (See Appendix I) The Basij is a passive defense civil militia that also serves as an indoctrination tool and is linked to a significant portion of Iran's human rights abuses.

Taken together, these 27 companies are worth more than 20% of the TSE, and are valued at $16.5 billion.[22] Former senior IRGC commanders who have never been subjected to sanctions sit on their boards. These estimates do not account for the hundreds of non-publicly-traded companies in which the IRGC holds controlling stakes.

Automotive Sector

The U.S. Treasury targeted Tehran's automotive sector in June 2013. Then-Undersecretary of the Treasury for Terrorism and Finance Intelligence David Cohen explained that the sector "is a significant contributor to its overall economic activity, generating funds that help prop up the rial and the regime."[23] In January 2014, the interim Joint Plan of Action agreement suspended sanctions against the automotive sector. With the signing of the JCPOA, however, that industry is set to further benefit in two significant ways:

- Easier access to dual-use technology for the automotive sector, which will also benefit from the general improvement of the economy

- Easier access to financing, foreign investment, and technology transfers

The automotive industry relies on dual-use technology, which includes fiber lasers for industrial welding and cutting,[24] electron-beam welding machines for automatic transmission systems,[25] flow-forming machines for rotational manufacture, and fiber-winding machines for the production of CNG pressure vessels and battery containers.[26] These technologies have applications in the aerospace, defense, and nuclear industries. Lifting bans on such exports is

(http://www.defenddemocracy.org/content/uploads/publications/FDDRoubini_Report_Irans_mysterious_shrinking_reserves.pdf)

[22] This number is their combined value on August 31, 2015 on the Tehran Stock Exchange (www.tse.ir). See more: Alexi Mostrous, Billy Kenber & Hugh Tomlinson, "Iranian Militia to Grab British Cash," *The Times* (U.K.), August 26, 2015. (http://www.thetimes.co.uk/tto/news/world/middleeast/article4538125.ece)

[23] U.S. Department of Treasury, Press Release. "Testimony Of Under Secretary for Terrorism And Financial Intelligence David Cohen Before The Senate Committee On Banking, Housing And Urban Affairs On 'Iran Sanctions: Ensuring Robust Enforcement, And Assessing Next Steps,'" June 4, 2013. (http://www.treasury.gov/press-center/press-releases/Pages/jl1969.aspx)

[24] James Harrington, "Dual-Use Technologies and Export Controls," *U.S. Department of State's Jefferson Science Lecture Series*, March 31, 2009. (http://www.state.gov/c/stas/series/154211.htm)

[25] "Electron Beam Welding Technology," *EBE Electron Beam Engineering Inc. Company Website*, accessed September 13, 2015. (http://www.ebeinc.com/Electron-Beam-Technology.html)

[26] "Entec Company Brochure," *Entec Composite Machines Inc. Company Website*, accessed September 13, 2015. (http://entec.com/Entec%20company%20brochure_final.pdf)

problematic, given the regime's significant presence in this sector and considering past cases of Iran's illicit procurement under the guise of automotive sector technology transfers.

In June 2013, the U.S. Treasury sanctioned a German factory, MCS International GmbH, along with its Iranian corporate owner – a religious foundation operating under the umbrella of EIKO.[27] MCS – a producer of cylinders for hybrid cars – held a flow-forming machine in its inventory that the regime sought to import to Iran shortly after buying the company in 2003.[28]

After German authorities denied them an export license, the Iranian owners of MCS frequently sent delegations of Iranian engineers for long periods to MCS in Germany. Eventually, they established a replica of the German factory in Iran, Pars MCS, which Treasury sanctioned in June 2013.

The IRGC is also active in the automotive sector, with five companies listed on the TSE: Bahman Group, Iran Tractor Manufacturing, Iran Tractor Foundry Company, Motorsazan Diesel and Gas Engines, and Iran Casting Industries.

Bahman Group is Iran's third largest carmaker and the proprietor of a license to produce Mazda cars for the domestic market. Bahman Group currently has a market value of approximately $300 million. It controls 24 companies,[29] including a share in Bahman Investment Co., another publicly traded company whose market value is currently estimated at around $80 million.[30] The board has five members, representing five companies. Four companies are IRGC-owned.[31]

The firm is a case study that illustrates how IRGC companies are structured to obfuscate corporate governance information as a means to evade sanctions. The two company shareholders that jointly control Bahman Group – Fan Pardazan Bahman Co. (27.41%) and Andishe Fardah Investment Company (25.62%)[32] – are both owned by Bahman Group itself. The identity of the board of directors, however, reveals IRGC control over the company.

[27] U.S. Department of Treasury, Press Release, "Treasury Targets Assets of Iranian Leadership," June 4, 2013. (http://www.treasury.gov/press-center/press-releases/Pages/jl1968.aspx)

[28] Michael Birnbaum & Joby Warrick, "A Mysterious Iranian-run Factory in Germany," *The Washington Post*, April 15, 2013. (https://www.washingtonpost.com/world/europe/a-mysterious-iranian-run-factory-in-germany/2013/04/15/92259d7a-a29f-11e2-82bc-511538ae90a4_story.html)

[29] "Ownership Status of Companies," *Bahman Group Company Website*, Accessed September 12, 2015. (http://www.bahmangroup.com/en/index.php/companies/ownership-status)

[30] Bahman Group owns 32.6% of Bahman Investment.

[31] "*Gorouh-e Bahman* (Bahman Group) – *Sahamdaran* (Shareholders)" *Tehran Stock Exchange*, accessed September 13, 2015. (http://new.tse.ir/Instrument.html?IRO1BHMN0001)

[32] "Corporate entry for Andishe Fardah Investment Co." *Iran Official Journal*, November 23, 2009. (http://www.gazette.ir/Detail.asp?NewsID=925341495024623&paperID=951869441925668)

Company Name	Registration Number	Previous Representative	Current Representative	National Identity Number	Position
Azerbaijan Diesel Vehicle Manufacturers Company (ADVMC)[33]	18527	Masih Mashhadi Tafreshi	Gholam Hossein Taghi Netaj Malekshah	5689642991	Chairman
Andisheh Mehvaran Investment Company (AMIC)[34]	203970	Mohammad Reza Soroush	Mohammad Reza Soroush	0569744441	Vice Chairman
Negin Royal Sahel Company (NRHC)[35]	322430	Mohammad Eskandari	Kazem Motamedifar	6439554832	Board Member
Tadbir Garan Atieh Iranian Investment (TAII)[36]	246077	Seyyed Mehdi Motevalian	Reza Asem Nakhjevani	0041160851	Board Member
Iran Credit Investment Company (ICIC)[37]	14046	Ali Rostami	Hadi Agha Babai		Board Member

Bahman Group and the firms that control it are IRGC companies. The same goes for Bahman Group's corporate governance and its 24 subsidiaries, many of which are 100% owned by Bahman Group, including 11 after-sales automobile services companies, five financial investment companies, three energy companies, three trading houses, and one car insurance company.[38] Bahman Group has thus far eluded designation, but it is still eligible for designation, even under the JCPOA. Failure to designate Bahman Group will only enrich the IRGC through Iran's automotive sector.

[33] ADVMC is a subsidiary of Iran Tractor Manufacturing Company – itself a subsidiary of Mehr Eghtesad Iranian Investment Company (MEIIC). The latter is a subsidiary of Mehr Eghtesad Bank, owned by the IRGC's Basij Cooperative Foundation and designated by Treasury on June 23, 2011; "*Sherkatha-ye Tabe* (Subsidiaries)," *Iran Tractor Manufacturing Group*, accessed September 2, 2015 (http://www.itm.co.ir/ps002t.aspx); and "*Darbare-ye Ma* (About Us)," *Iran Tractor Manufacturing Group*, accessed September 2, 2015.
(http://www.itm.co.ir/pi001t.aspx); Treasury's designation of Mehr Bank: U.S. Department of Treasury, Press Release, "Fact Sheet: Treasury Sanctions Major Iranian Commercial Entities," June 23, 2011.
(http://www.treasury.gov/press-center/press-releases/Pages/tg1217.aspx)
[34] AMIC is a subsidiary of Iran Zinc Mines Development Company, which is controlled by MEIIC. "*Sarmaye Gozari-ye Andishe Mehvaran* (Andisheh Mehvaran Investment), *Iran Zinc Mines Development Company*, accessed September 2, 2015. (http://izmdc.com/?page_id=121)
[35] NRHC's board members are MEII, TAII, and Tajalli Samane Investment Company. The latter is a subsidiary of IRGC-owned Mehr Eghtesad Iranian Brokerage Company. "*Agahiye Taghirat-e Sherkat-e Negin Sahel Royal* (Change Bulletin for Negin Sahel Royal Company)," *Iranian Official Journal*, January 13, 2013.
(http://www.gazette.ir/Detail.asp?NewsID=917412606859553&paperID=916206452817003); and *Darbare-ye Ma* (About Us), *Mehr Eghtesad Iranian Brokerage Company Website*, accessed September 2, 2015.
(http://meibourse.com/?tabid=381)
[36] TAII is a subsidiary of MEIIC: "*Sherkat-e Tadbirgaran-e Atieh* (Tadbirgaran Atieh Company)," *Mehr Eghtesad Bank*, accessed September 2, 2015. (http://mebank.ir/index.aspx?siteid=1&pageid=207)
[37] ICIC was, until recently, a subsidiary of Bahman Group.
[38] "Ownership Status of Companies," *Bahman Group Company Website*, Accessed September 12, 2015.
(http://www.bahmangroup.com/en/index.php/companies/ownership-status)

Oil, Gas, and Petrochemical Sectors

The IRGC will benefit from the end of sanctions against Iran's energy sector in two ways:

- IRGC firms already own important contracts across the entire sector and will win more as foreign capital and technology return to Iran's energy industry.

- The JCPOA will permanently remove barriers to trade in the petrochemical sector, allowing renewed Iranian access to sensitive dual-use technology.

The lifting of energy sanctions will enable Iran to draw investment and foreign companies for both upstream and downstream projects. The Iranian energy sector is also going to benefit from access to Western technology that was previously restricted by EU sanctions– including liquid natural gas technology, refining, and petrochemicals production. IRGC companies now stand to gain from Iran's state-owned energy companies' ability to issue bonds to finance projects, and from the ability of delisted state companies to procure technology for these projects.

South Pars, a vast natural gas field, is a case in point. After EU sanctions pushed European companies out of the field in late 2010, contracts eventually went to IRGC subsidiaries like the Sepanir Oil and Gas Development Company. Sepanir was sanctioned in June 2010 under UN Security Council Resolution 1929, and the U.S. Treasury added it to its list of IRGC-designated entities the same month.[39] EU sanctions against Iran's natural gas sector prevented access to technology critical for the development of the project.

These restrictions are set to change under the JCPOA, even as Sepanir will remain under U.S. sanctions, and until Transition Day, will remain under EU sanctions. Much of the procurement and manufacturing of technology is being conducted by Mapna Boiler Co.,[40] a subsidiary of the Iranian giant Mapna Group, which is under neither EU nor U.S. sanctions, despite being designated by Canada[41] and the United Kingdom[42] for its ties to the Islamic Republic of Iran's prohibited nuclear and ballistic missile programmes.[43]

---

[39] U.S. Department of Treasury, Press Release, "Fact Sheet: U.S. Treasury Department Targets Iran's Nuclear and Missile Programs," June 16, 2010. (http://www.treasury.gov/press-center/press-releases/Pages/tg747.aspx)

[40] "Project's Name: South Pars (Phase 15 & 16)," *Projects Website, Mapna Boiler and Equipment Engineering and Manufacturing Company*, accessed September 13, 2015.
(http://www.mapnaboiler.com/Projects/MapnaBoilerProjects/tabid/258/agentType/View/PropertyID/68/Default.aspx)

[41] "Special Economic Measures (Iran) Regulations" SOR/2010-165. Amended Version, May 29, 2013. (http://laws-lois.justice.gc.ca/eng/regulations/sor-2010-165/fulltext.html)

[42] Department for Business Innovation & Skills, Export Control Organization, "Guidance Iran List," November 19, 2013. (https://www.gov.uk/government/publications/iran-list/iran-list)

[43] One of Mapna's subsidiaries, Mapna Turbine Blade Manufacturing Engineering Co., was cited as the end-user for a procurement of dual-use technology in the June 2014 report of the UN Panel of Experts in charge of reporting on the implementation of UN Security Council resolution 1929. Panel of Experts established pursuant to Security Council resolution 1929, United Nations. "Final report of the Panel of Experts established pursuant to resolution 1929 (2010)" June 5, 2014, page 13. (http://www.securitycouncilreport.org/atf/cf/%7B65BFCF9B-6D27-4E9C-8CD3-CF6E4FF96FF9%7D/S_2014_394.pdf)

Mapna has an extensive network of overseas procurement offices.[44] Their ability to expand procurement and help Sepanir is assured by the lifting of sectorial sanctions, which will begin on Implementation Day.

Similarly, the lifting of oil sanctions, including access to sector-specific technology, will benefit the IRGC-owned National Iran Oil Company (NIOC) and its many subsidiaries, which the EU is set to delist on Implementation Day. For example, the South Yaran oil field, a project owned by NIOC's subsidiary the Petroleum Engineering Development Company (PEDEC). Production at South Yaran is set to begin in mid-2016 and will yield approximately 50,000 barrels per day.[45] According to *Fars News*, "National Iranian Drilling Company (NIDC), Puya Energy Kish, Naft Kar and Khatam al-Anbia Construction Headquarters are in charge of drilling."[46] These are all IRGC companies that stand to gain experience and contracts, as Iran seeks to make up for lost time and investment in its energy sector.

Iran's petrochemical products are, after oil, the country's largest source of foreign income and its second-leading export. While not a majority owner in any of the petrochemical companies publicly traded on the TSE, the IRGC holds major stakes in:

- Kermanshah Petrochemical Industries Co. (market value: $362.6 million)[47]

- Pardis Petrochemical Co. (market value: $1.62 billion)[48]

- Parsian Oil & Gas Development Co. (market value: $2.6 billion)[49]

- Shiraz Petrochemical Co. (market value: $527.8 million)[50]

---

[44] Mapna International FZE (UAE), Mapna International Shanghai (China), Mapna Europe GmbH (Germany), Mapna Italia srl (Italy), Energy Trading Elctrik Sanayi ve Ticaret Limited Sirketi and Ms Uluslararası Enerji Yatırım Anonim Şirketi (Turkey), and Kura Industrial Trading LLC (Republic of Georgia). Corporate entries for Mapna Europe GmbH are available at Germany's commercial registry portal (www.handelsregister.de); Mapna Italia are available at Italy's commercial registry (www.registroimprese.it); Mapna subsidiaries in Turkey are available from the website of Istanbul's Chamber of Commerce (www.ito.org.tr); entries for Kura Industrial Trading LLC, showing that Kura is a wholly owned subsidiary of Eletrik Sanayi are available from the official Georgian commercial registry (http://enreg.reestri.gov.ge).

[45] "Drilling of South Yaran Oil Field Kicked Off," *Petroleum Engineering and Development Company*, August 1, 2013. (http://pedec.ir/en/detail=2510)

[46] "South Yaran Operational by March 2016," *Fars News*, August 3, 2015. (http://english.farsnews.com/newstext.aspx?nn=13940511000976)

[47] "*Sanaye Petrochimi-e Kermanshah* (Kermanshah Petrochemical Industries) – *Sahamdaran* (Shareholders)" *Tehran Securities Exchange Technology Management Company*, accessed September 13, 2015. (http://www.tsetmc.com/Loader.aspx?ParTree=151311&i=38437201078089290#).

[48] "*Petrochimi-ye Pardis* (Pardis Petrochemical) – *Sahamdaran* (Shareholders)," *Tehran Securities Exchange Technology Management Company*, accessed September 13, 2015. (http://www.tsetmc.com/Loader.aspx?ParTree=151311&i=20562694899904339#)

[49] "*Gostaresh Naft va-Gaz Parsian* (Parsian Oil and Gas Development Co.) – *Sahamdaran* (Shareholders)," *Tehran Securities Exchange Technology Management Company*, accessed September 13, 2015. (http://www.tsetmc.com/Loader.aspx?ParTree=151311&i=23441366113375722#)

Revenue from dividends and interest generated by these investments goes to pay retirement funds, insurance, and social security for military personnel and their families. Growth in revenue from these investments means assured resources to support members of the IRGC – including the Quds Force and Basij – and their families.

The Guards can also benefit from the lifting of sanctions against technology transfers to Iran, especially given their dual-use applications.

Western sanctions against Iran's petrochemical sector date back to the United Nations Security Council Resolution 1929 in 2010.[51] In its preamble, UNSCR 1929 noted:

> "[T]he potential connection between Iran's revenues derived from its energy sector and the funding of Iran's proliferation-sensitive nuclear activities, and *further noting* that chemical process equipment and materials required for the petrochemical industry have much in common with those required for certain sensitive nuclear fuel cycle activities."

The European Union sanctioned Iran's petrochemical sector in March 2012. EU sanctions targeted both Iranian exports of petrochemical products (as well as associated services) and Iranian imports of technology for the petrochemical sector. The U.S. Treasury blacklisted eight Iranian petrochemical companies in May 2013.[52]

The November 2013 Joint Plan of Action interim agreement suspended sanctions against Iranian exports of petrochemicals, enabling 14 companies to sell their products.[53] That agreement left in place sanctions against Iranian purchases of technology. The JCPOA will give Iranian petrochemical companies, including those owned by the IRGC, access to sensitive dual-use technology.

---

[50] "*Petrochimi-e Shiraz* (Shiraz Petrochemical) – *Sahamdaran* (Shareholders)," *Tehran Securities Exchange Technology Management Company*, accessed September 13, 2015.
(http://www.tsetmc.com/Loader.aspx?ParTree=151311&i=38568786927478796#)
[51] United Nations Security Council, "Resolution 1929 (2010)," June 9, 2010.
(http://www.un.org/en/ga/search/view_doc.asp?symbol=S/RES/1929%282010%29)
[52] U.S. Department of Treasury, Press Release, "U.S. Announces New Sanctions against Iran" May 31, 2013 (http://www.treasury.gov/press-center/press-releases/Pages/jl1965.aspx); U.S. Department of State, Spokesperson, "Companies Sanctioned under Iran Sanctions Authorities," May 31, 2013.
(http://www.state.gov/r/pa/prs/ps/2013/05/210147.htm)
[53] U.S. Department of State, Office of the Spokesperson, "Guidance Relating to the Provision of Certain Temporary Sanctions Relief in Order to Implement the Joint Plan of Action Reached on November 24, 2013, Between the P5+1 and the Islamic Republic of Iran," January 20, 2014.
(http://www.state.gov/p/nea/rls/220049.htm); The companies were: (1) Bandar Imam Petrochemical Company; (2) Bou Ali Sina Petrochemical Company; (3) Ghaed Bassir Petrochemical Products Company; (4) Iran Petrochemical Commercial Company; (5) Jam Petrochemical Company; (6) Marjan Petrochemical Company; (7) Mobin Petrochemical Company; (8) National Petrochemical Company; (9) Nouri Petrochemical Company; (10) Pars Petrochemical Company; (11) Sadaf Petrochemical Assaluyeh Company; (12) Shahid Tondgooyan Petrochemical Company; (13) Shazand Petrochemical Company; and (14) Tabriz Petrochemical Company. Ghaed Bassir Petrochemical Products Company is a subsidiary of the Headquarters of the Execution of the Imam Khomeini Order.

Metals and Minerals

Iran's mining sector is an important source of revenue for the country's economy as well as a supplier of raw materials for its developing industry. According to the Organization for Investment Economic and Technical Assistance of Iran, "Iran has the world's largest zinc reserves and second-largest reserves of copper." [54]

The publicly traded Iran Zinc Mines Development Company (IZMDCO) is the principal owner and producer of Iranian zinc, with an $80-million market value and control of an important chunk of the country's extractive activities. With the lifting of sanctions against the Islamic Republic's banking and transport sectors, Iranian metals and minerals exports will become a more affordable option for international buyers. IZMDCO, which is majority-owned by the IRGC, [55] will thus benefit from the general climate of economic improvement, access to modern extraction technology, financing, cheaper delivery costs, and potentially foreign investment.

The metallurgic sector is also critical to Iran's economic health. Iran's largest aluminum producer, Iran Aluminum Company or IRALCO, was sanctioned by the European Union in December 2012 because it assisted "designated entities to violate the provisions of UN and EU sanctions on Iran and is directly supporting Iran's proliferation sensitive nuclear activities. As of mid-2012 IRALCO had a contract to supply aluminum to EU-designated Iran Centrifuge Technology Company." [56] Because IRALCO was sanctioned for nuclear-related activities alone, the EU will delist it on Implementation Day. The U.S. never designated IRALCO, and therefore has no secondary sanctions against the firm. According to IRALCO's July 2015 report, the IRGC-owned (and U.S.-sanctioned) Mehr Eghtesad Iranian Investment owns 20% of the company. [57]

IRALCO, which supplied the Iranian nuclear program with aluminum to build centrifuges – and whose revenues help fill the IRGC's financial coffers – is now slated to benefit from the economic boom the JCPOA will generate.

---

[54] "Industry and Mining – Overview" *Invest in Iran/Organization for Investment Economic and Technical Assistance of Iran website*, accessed September 13, 2015. (http://www.investiniran.ir/en/sectors/industry)

[55] *"Toseyeh Ma'adan Rouyeh Iran – Sahamdaran* (Iran Zinc Mines Development Company - Shareholders)," *Tehran Securities Exchange Technology Management Company*, accessed September 13, 2015. (http://www.tsetmc.com/Loader.aspx?ParTree=151311&i=22787503301679573); The IRGC owns a combined 51.8% of IZMDCO through five companies: Mehr Eghtesad Financial Group (18.4%), Mehr Eghtesad Iranian Investment Company (18.39%), Tadbir Garan Atieh Iranian Investment Company (9.11%), Negin Sahel Royal Company (3.26%), and the mineral company Calcimin (2.65%).

[56] "Council Implementing Regulation (EU) No 1264/2012 of 21 December 2012 implementing Regulation (EU) No 267/2012 concerning restrictive measures against Iran," *Official Journal of the European Union*, December 22, 2012, page 356/57, entry No. 6. (http://eur-lex.europa.eu/LexUriServ/LexUriServ.do?uri=OJ:L:2012:356:0055:0060:en:PDF)

[57] Treasury sanctioned Mehr Eghtesad for being owned by Mehr Bank, another subsidiary of the IRGC. U.S. Department of Treasury, Press Release, "Fact Sheet: Treasury Sanctions Major Iranian Commercial Entities," June 23, 2011 (http://www.treasury.gov/press-center/press-releases/Pages/tg1217.aspx); and U.S Department of Treasury, Press Release, "Fact Sheet: Treasury Designates Iranian Entities Tied to the IRGC and IRISL," December 21, 2010. (http://www.treasury.gov/press-center/press-releases/Pages/tg1010.aspx)

Telecommunications

Another sector where the IRGC is bound to reap economic benefits is telecommunications. The IRGC controls Iran's largest telecom company, the Telecommunication Company of Iran or TCI.[58] The Guards bought the formerly government-owned company in September 2009 in a controversial bid that at the last minute disqualified the only non-IRGC offer.[59] TCI's main shareholder is now Toseye Etemad Mobin (50%), a company controlled by the IRGC jointly with the supreme leader's financial network, through two companies – the Tadbir Group-owned Gostaresh Electronic Mobin and Shahriar Mahestan Company.

TCI has a monopoly over Iran's landlines, and thus controls much of the country's Internet traffic. As *Al-Monitor* reported in August 2013, all three mobile operators in Iran are directly or indirectly partners with IRGC-affiliated companies. [60]

The IRGC will also now be in a position to benefit from sensitive monitoring technology it can put to its advantage to enhance its surveillance abilities against the country's dissidents. *Reuters* reported in 2012 that China's ZTE Corporation sold TCI "a powerful surveillance system capable of monitoring landline, mobile and internet communications."[61] TCI was never sanctioned by the U.S. or EU, either for its IRGC ownership or potential role in humanrights violations. Instead, the U.S. Department of State in 2013 designated an IRGC-subsidiary, Ofogh Saberin Engineering Development Company, under Executive Order 13628, for its "material support to censorship or other activities" in the 2009 security crackdown.[62] The subsidiary remains under sanctions, but the State Department did not explicitly identify the firm as an IRGC firm.

Iran's telecom sector will attract foreign investment and gain significant access to advanced technology. The IRGC will thus increase revenue, as well as its ability to spy on and censor its citizens, under the JCPOA.

---

[58] Michael Slackman. "Elite Guard in Iran Tightens Grip with Media Move." *The New York Times*, October 8, 2009. (http://www.nytimes.com/2009/10/09/world/middleeast/09iran.html?_r=0)

[59] Robin Wright, editor, *The Iran Primer*, (Washington, DC: United States Institute of Peace, 2010), page 55.

[60] Khourosh Avaei. "What to expect in Iran's Telecom Sector." *Al-Monitor*, August 18, 2013. (http://www.al-monitor.com/pulse/originals/2013/08/expect-iran-telecom-sector.html#)

[61] Steve Stecklow, "Special Report: Chinese Firm helps Iran spy on its Citizens," *Reuters*, 22 March 2012. (http://www.reuters.com/article/2012/03/22/us-iran-telecoms-idUSBRE82L0B820120322)

[62] U.S. Department of State. Office of the Spokesperson. "United States Takes Action to Facilitate Communications by the Iranian People and Targets Iranian Government Censorship," May 30, 2013. (http://www.state.gov/r/pa/prs/ps/2013/05/210102.htm)

Transport

The IRGC is also set to benefit from the lifting of sanctions against the transport sector in three ways:

- The IRGC has relied on Iran's largest shipping and aviation companies – including the state-owned Islamic Republic of Iran Shipping Lines (IRISL) and its subsidiaries, and the state-owned Iran Air[63] – to carry military equipment and personnel to proxies abroad. Both companies are now being delisted by the U.S. and EU.[64]

- The U.S. commitment to lift restrictions on sales of aircraft, spare parts, and maintenance services will allow the Iran Air fleet – which the U.S. Treasury sanctioned as an accessory to war crimes in Syria – to improve the quality and reliability of its air services to its customers, including the IRGC.

- The IRGC controls and manages most Iranian commercial ports. Although its biggest port operator, Tidewater Middle East PLC, remains under U.S. and EU sanctions until Transition Day, the inevitable increase in shipping prompted by the lifting of sanctions will enrich IRGC-owned companies managing container terminals and port services.

- The IRGC is involved in transportation-related infrastructure projects nationwide including railway networks, port expansion, highway improvement, and high-velocity trains. The lifting of sanctions will provide better access to financing, technology transfers, and international partners for these IRGC projects.

Recent contracts issued by the Islamic Republic of Iran Railways illustrate how it is impossible to insulate the IRGC from the lifting of sectorial bans. In February 2015, work began on a $2.7-billion project to link Tehran to Isfahan by high-speed railway. The project is spearheaded by the China Railway Engineering Corporation, together with the U.S.-, EU-, and UN-sanctioned construction giant Khatam al-Anbiya. Financing will come partially from Iran's Bank of Industry

---

[63] According to Treasury, "Iran Air has shipped military-related equipment on behalf of the IRGC since 2006, and in September and November 2008, Iran Air shipped aircraft-related raw materials to a MODAFL-associated company, including titanium sheets, which have dual-use military applications and can be used in support of advanced weapons programs. Rockets or missiles have been transported via Iran Air passenger aircraft, and IRGC officers occasionally take control over Iran Air flights carrying special IRGC-related cargo. The IRGC is also known to disguise and manifest such shipments as medicine and generic spare parts, and IRGC officers have discouraged Iran Air pilots from inspecting potentially dangerous IRGC-related cargo being carried aboard a commercial Iran Air aircraft, including to Syria. Additionally, commercial Iran Air flights have also been used to transport missile or rocket components to Syria;" U.S. Department of Treasury, Press Release, "Fact Sheet: Treasury Sanctions Major Iranian Commercial Entities" June 23, 2011. (http://www.treasury.gov/press-center/press-releases/Pages/tg1217.aspx).
[64] U.S. Department of Treasury, Press Release, "Fact Sheet: Treasury Sanctions Major Iranian Commercial Entities,"
June 23, 2011. (http://www.treasury.gov/press-center/press-releases/Pages/tg1217.aspx).

and Mine,[65] a government-owned entity that the U.S. Treasury sanctioned in 2011[66] and the EU sanctioned in 2012, but which will be removed from both sanctions lists on Implementation Day.

A few days before the JCPOA was signed, Iran's railways authorities announced another deal to revamp train stations in Tehran, Qom, and Mashhad.[67] The contract, awarded to French state-owned company AREP, is part of a $25-billion project to modernize Iran's railways. In the words of Mohsen Pourseyed-Aqa'ie, the head of the Islamic Republic of Iran Railways, "All the contracting work for construction and upgrades would be carried out by Iranian companies, with outside companies brought in for design work and other kinds of consultancy."[68] We can expect IRGC firms to benefit.

The lifting of aviation restrictions poses other challenges. Under Section 5.1.1 of the JCPOA's Annex II, Washington will "allow for the sale of commercial passenger aircraft and related parts and services to Iran," as well as the export, lease, and transfer of aircraft, and the provision of associated services to aircraft, provided they are "for exclusively civil aviation end-use."[69]

This provision is designed to allow Iranian airlines to modernize their aging fleet[70] while warning them of the risks involved in serving as fronts for entities still on Treasury's Specially Designated Nationals (SDN) list and in lending their planes for logistical support of terrorism abroad. Iranian airlines like Mahan Air and Yas Air, which Washington has targeted for ferrying weapons and personnel to Syria, will remain under U.S. sanctions. On Implementation Day, however, the U.S. will delist Aban Air, Iran Air, and Iranair Tours – three other Iranian airlines previously involved in such conduct.

Aban Air was designated under Executive Order 13382 in May 2013 for providing support to Iran Air and the IRGC. According to Treasury, "the IRGC used Aban Air to clandestinely ship cargo to and from Iran."[71] Yet Aban Air, according to the JCPOA, will be able to modernize its fleet without any guarantee that it will not engage in similar activities in the future.

---

[65] Iran's Bank of Industry and Mine, Press Release. "President Rouhani Officially Starts Tehran-Isfahan High-Speed Rail Project," March 3, 2015. (http://en.bim.ir/detail/p10088872.bim)

[66] U.S. Department of Treasury, Press Release, "Treasury Designates Iranian State-Owned Bank for Facilitating Iran's Proliferation Activities," May 17, 2011.
(http://www.treasury.gov/press-center/press-releases/Pages/tg1178.aspx)

[67] David Rogers, "French Transport Consultant Wins First Contract in $25bn Iranian Rail programme." *Global Construction Review*, July 6, 2015. (http://www.globalconstructionreview.com/news/french-transp8rt-con6su0l6t4a2nt8-0w6i4n2s-fi8r8st/.)

[68] David Rogers, "French transport Consultant Wins First Contract in $25bn Iranian Rail programme." *Global Construction Review*, July 6, 2015, http://www.globalconstructionreview.com/news/french-transp8rt-con6su0l6t4a2nt8-0w6i4n2s-fi8r8st/.

[69] "Joint Comprehensive Plan of Action – Annex II – Sanctions related commitments." July 14, 2015, Section 5.1.1. (http://eeas.europa.eu/statements-eeas/docs/iran_agreement/annex_2_sanctions_related_commitments_en.pdf)

[70] Aaron S. Goldblatt & Roozbeh Aliabadi, "How Sanctions Relief will impact Iran's Civil Aviation Industry," *The Hill*, June 5, 2014. (http://thehill.com/blogs/congress-blog/foreign-policy/208085-how-sanctions-relief-will-impact-irans-civil-aviation)

[71] U.S. Department of Treasury, Press Release, "Treasury Announces New Sanctions against Iran," May 23, 2013. (http://www.treasury.gov/press-center/press-releases/Pages/jl1955.aspx)

Iran Air and Iran Air Tours (a subsidiary of Iran Air) were both designated in 2011 under Executive Order 13382.[72] According to Treasury, their practices, including "disguis[ing]…weapons shipments as medicine and generic spare parts" to Syria, are in clear contravention of international aviation safety standards. However, Iran Air's support for the IRGC's ongoing war efforts in Syria did not keep these two airlines listed.

Yas Air (now called Pouya Air), which will remain under sanctions, was designated in 2012 under Executive Order 13224 for acting "on behalf of the IRGC-QF [Quds Force] to transport illicit cargo – including weapons – to Iran's clients in the Levant."[73] According to Treasury, Yas Air "has moved IRGC-QF personnel and weapons under the cover of humanitarian aid."[74]

Mahan Air, which will also remain sanctioned under the JCPOA, was designated in October 2011 under Executive Order 13224 "for providing financial, material and technological support" to the Quds Force, including ferrying personnel and weapons to Syria. [75] That involvement in Syria appears to continue. In September 2015, two Mahan Air aircraft flew from Tehran to Abadan and, after a quick stopover, continued to Syria.[76] The first landed in Damascus and the second in Latakia (see images below), where the IRGC reportedly has a military base. Neither flight is advertised by the airline or can be purchased by regular passengers.

Remarkably, because only the U.S. sanctions will remain, Mahan Air can fly to more than a dozen European destinations and has recently announced the expansion of its European routes,[77] with the airline servicing some destinations with planes it acquired last May in violation of U.S. sanctions.[78]

---

[72] U.S. Department of Treasury, Press Release, "Fact Sheet: Treasury Sanctions Major Iranian Commercial Entities," June 23, 2011. (http://www.treasury.gov/press-center/press-releases/Pages/tg1217.aspx)

[73] U.S. Department of Treasury, Press Release, "Treasury Targets Iranian Arms Shipments," March 27, 2012. (http://www.treasury.gov/press-center/press-releases/Pages/tg1506.aspx)

[74] U.S. Department of Treasury, Press Release, "Treasury Designates Syrian Entity, Others Involved in Arms and Communications Procurement Networks and Identifies Blocked Iranian Aircraft," September 19, 2012. (http://www.treasury.gov/press-center/press-releases/Pages/tg1714.aspx)

[75] U.S. Department of Treasury, Press Release, "Treasury Designates Iranian Commercial Airline Linked to Iran's Support for Terrorism," October 12, 2011. (http://www.treasury.gov/press-center/press-releases/Pages/tg1322.aspx)

[76] The aircraft registration numbers were EP-MNT and EP-MNV.

[77] The new routes are: Tehran-Moscow, Tehran-St. Petersburg, Tehran-Sochi, Tehran-Athens and Tehran-Milan: "Mahan Air announces six new international routes" CAPA Center for Aviation Website, May 20, 2015. (http://centreforaviation.com/members/direct-news/mahan-air-opens-6-new-international-routes-from-may-142015-225574)

[78] U.S. Department of Treasury, Press Release, "Treasury Department Targets Those Involved in Iranian Scheme to Purchase Airplanes," May 21, 2015. (http://www.treasury.gov/press-center/press-releases/Pages/jl10061.aspx). According to data available on the commercial website www.flightradar24.com, Mahan's sanctioned aircraft tail registration EP-MMH flew into Athens on 6 September, 2015; EP-MMI flew into Munich on September 2, 2015.

Image 1: Mahan Air aircraft EP-MNT flies to Latakia (September 4, 2015)

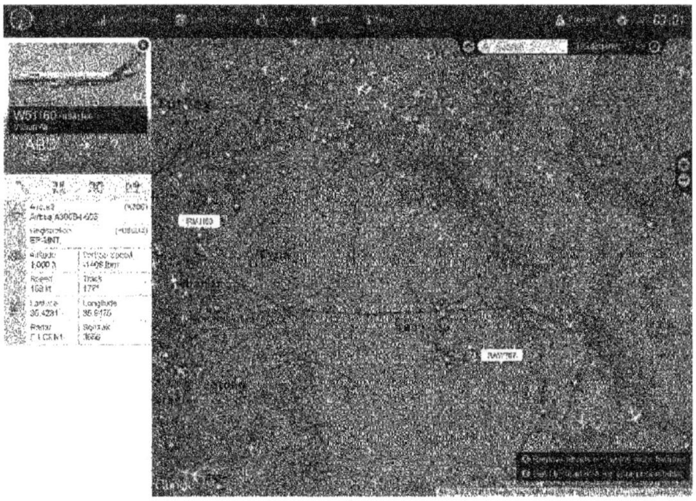

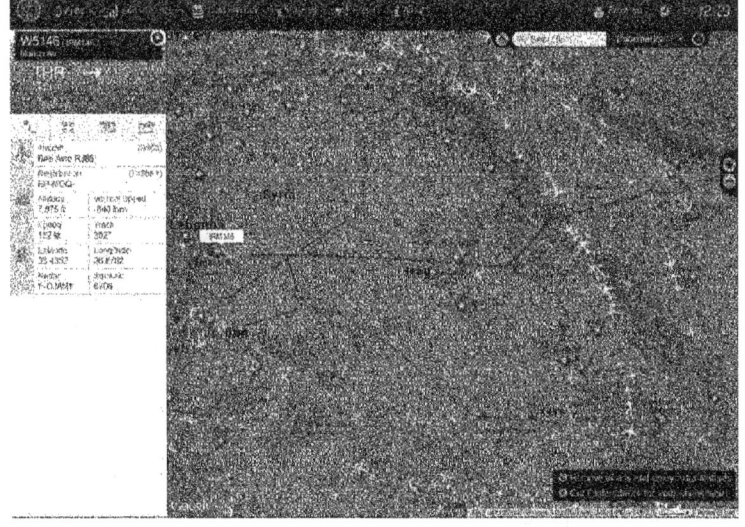

A screenshot from FlightRadar24, a commercial flight tracker, shows Mahan Air's EP-MNT flight path from Tehran to Abadan and onto Latakia in the early morning hours of September 4, 2015.

Image 2: Mahan Air aircraft EP-MOQ lands in Damascus (September 14, 2015)

A screenshot from FlightRadar24, a commercial flight tracker, shows Mahan Air's EP-MOQ flight path from Tehran to Damascus in the afternoon of September 14, 2015.

Construction

The IRGC construction arm, Khatam al-Anbiya, employs over 135,000 people, works with over 5,000 contractors, and reportedly has over 800 reported subsidiaries.[79] Among its projects are 51 contracts with the Oil Ministry worth more than $17 billion;[80] the $2-billion Bakhtiari Dam[81] – slated to be the tallest in the world; the $3-billion "shrine-to-shrine" highway[82] connecting Qom and Mashhad; and a Tehran metro line that is part of a $7-billion metro-expansion program.[83]

Sepasad, one of Khatam al-Anbiya's subsidiaries, is developing several metro projects to lengthen and improve commuters' connections to Tehran and its international airport from satellite towns. It is also the contractor for the Moshampa Dam.[84]

The anticipated increase in public spending to modernize and improve Iran's aging infrastructure will no doubt lead to public tenders for large projects. KAA will be the primary beneficiary. While the Obama Administration may be correct in noting that the bulk of the $100 billion in sanctions relief will flow to construction projects and not go directly to terrorist proxies, it is reasonable to assume that much of it will flow through the IRGC's construction arms and thereforemake its way to terrorist coffers.

Banking and financial Provisions

On Implementation Day, the European Union will:

- Delist most Iranian banks that it sanctioned over the past decade

- Lift restrictions on banking transactions to and from Iran, including the €40,000 cap per transaction and the obligation to report and authorize transactions

- Lift restrictions on messaging services for financial transactions, thereby allowing the return of most Iranian banks to the SWIFT network

- Lift restrictions on financial support for trade with Iran

- Lift restrictions on Iranian government public-guaranteed bonds[85]

---

[79] Massimo Calabresi, "New Iranian Sanctions Target Revolutionary Guards," *Time Magazine*, June 10, 2010. (http://content.time.com/time/magazine/article/0,9171,1995869,00.html)

[80] Nargas Rasooli, "*51 Gharardad bein Vezarae Naft va Majmooe-ye Khatam Basteh Shod* (51 Contracts Signed between the Ministry of Petroleum and Khatam al-Anbiya)," *Magiran*, May 23, 2012. (http://www.magiran.com/npview.asp?ID=2507886)

[81] "Bakhtiari Project – Project Introduction," *Iran Power & Water Resources Development Company Website*, accessed September 13, 2015. (http://en.iwpco.ir/Bakhtiari/default.aspx)

[82] "Shrine to Shrine Highway Project Starts," *Press TV*, October 10, 2010. (http://edition.presstv.ir/detail/145999.html)

[83] Ladane Nasseri, "Tehran to End Initial $7 Billion Metro Expansion by March," *Bloomberg*, October 22, 2014. (http://www.bloomberg.com/news/articles/2014-10-22/tehran-to-end-initial-7-billion-metro-expansion-by-march)

[84] "*Projeh Sad Mahzani va Band Tansimi Moshampa* (Moshampa Dam Construction Project)," *Sepasad Company Website* accessed September 13, 2015. (http://www.sepasad.ir/fa/index.php/moshampa-dam-project)

The U.S. will also move to terminate financial sanctions against most Iranian financial institutions. However, these banks will remain subject to restrictions for U.S. persons. According to the JCPOA, "U.S. persons and foreign entities owned or controlled by a U.S. person will continue to be prohibited from transactions with these individuals and entities, pursuant to the Iranian Transactions and Sanctions Regulations."[86]

The rest of the world, however, will be able to interact with these financial institutions. By allowing these banks to reconnect to the global financial system and lifting restrictions on their operations, the agreement will allow all unsanctioned IRGC companies to regain access to the global financial system by using delisted banks to transact their business. That is sufficient to enable the Guards to resume banking operations in Europe. Iranian banks, in turn, will be able to raise capital through Iranian government public-guaranteed bonds, which will finance public projects contracted to IRGC companies.[87] Finally, as Iran's economy improves, IRGC investment firms' portfolios will grow as a result.

The U.S.-sanctioned Mehr Eghtesad Iranian Investment Company is one illustrative case. In addition to its aforementioned role as a major shareholder of IRALCO, Iran's largest aluminum producer, the firm also has shares in Isfahan Mobarakeh Steel,[88] Tecnotar,[89] and the Zinc Mines Development Company.[90] Mehr Eghtesad may still be sanctioned, but its investments are not. There is no way the JCPOA can prevent the company from cashing in on its investments and using revenue from them to fund IRGC military activities.

There are also IRGC investment firms that are *not* sanctioned, like Tadbir Garan Atieh Iranian Investment Company. Not only will these companies now increase their income from investments, but they will also be able to invest their assets abroad as well.[91]

---

[85] "Joint Comprehensive Plan of Action, Annex II – Sanctions-related commitments." Vienna, July 14, 2015. (http://eeas.europa.eu/statements-eeas/docs/iran_agreement/annex_2_sanctions_related_commitments_en.pdf)

[86] These are the entities marked by an asterisk in Annex II, Attachment 3, of the JCPOA: "Joint Comprehensive Plan of Action, Annex II – Attachments." Vienna, July 14, 2015, Attachment 3. page 1. (http://eeas.europa.eu/statements-eeas/docs/iran_agreement/annex_1_attachements_en.pdf)

[87] Iran has already announced a $1.7 billion bond issue for the current calendar year to help finance energy sector projects: "Iran to sell bonds for key energy plans," *Press TV*, August 25, 2015. (http://www.presstv.com/Detail/2015/08/25/426235/Iran-to-sell-bonds-for-key-energy-plans)

[88] "*Foolad-e Mobarakeh Isfahan* (Isfahan Mobarakeh Steel)," *Tehran Stock Exchange*, accessed September 15, 2015. (http://new.tse.ir/Instrument.html?IRO1FOLD0001)

[89] "Technotar – *Sahamdaran* (Shareholders)," *Tehran Stock Exchange*, accessed September 13, 2015. (http://new.tse.ir/Instrument.html?IRO1TKNO0001)

[90] "*Toseyeh Ma'adan Rouyeh Iran* (Iran Zinc Mines Development Co.) – *Sahamdaran* (Shareholders)," *Tehran Stock Exchange*, accessed September 13, 2015. (http://new.tse.ir/Instrument.html?IRO1ROOI0001)

[91] It owns shares in Zinc Mines Development Company, Exir Pharmaceutical, Behbahan Cement, Sina Kashi and Ceramic, Rayan Saipa Leasing, Isfahan Oil Refinery and Kaveh Paper Industries. Their corporate entries can be found here: "*Darousazi Exir* (Exir Pharmaceutical) – *Sahamdaran* (Shareholders)," *Tehran Stock Exchange*, accessed September 13, 2015. http://new.tse.ir/Instrument.html?IRO1EXIR0001; "*Sanaye Kaghzesazi Kaveh* (Kaveh Paper Industries) – *Sahamdaran* (Shareholders)," *Tehran Stock Exchange*, accessed September 13, 2015. (http://new.tse.ir/Instrument.html?IRO1KSKA0001); "*Palayesh Naft Esfahan* (Isfahan Oil Refinery) – *Sahamdaran* (Shareholders)," *Tehran Stock Exchange*, accessed September 13, 2015.

IRGC Entities that Eluded Sanctions

Most IRGC-linked companies were never identified as such by EU or U.S. authorities. Companies not designated by U.S., EU, or UN are now likely to benefit from the economic windfall because the international business community will presume that Iranian companies not listed are legitimate business partners. These include both publicly traded and private companies, which can now benefit from the lifting of sanctions in three ways:

- Trade with Western purchasers and procure technology from Western suppliers, including dual-use technology

- Renewed ability to gain access to financial services, including the ability to invest in foreign securities

- General economic improvement in the country, facilitating new contracts and public tenders

These companies will also now be able to send senior executives – many of them former IRGC commanders – to represent them overseas.

Technically speaking, subsidiaries of designated companies are all under sanctions, and no company or financial institution is likely to risk transacting with an entity on a U.S. or EU sanctions list. In theory, Iranian entities that are not listed may still draw enhanced scrutiny from anti-money laundering and compliance authorities. In practice, however, the global business community looks to the U.S. Treasury for guidance and will assume that what is not explicitly forbidden is allowed.

Treasury has acknowledged this role. When on February 20, 2010, Treasury designated[92] a number of subsidiaries of the IRGC's construction conglomerate Khatam al-Anbiya, then-Undersecretary of Treasury for Terror Finance Intelligence, Stuart Levy, said that "Today's action exposing Khatam al-Anbiya subsidiaries will help firms worldwide avoid business that ultimately benefits the IRGC and its dangerous activities."[93]

The IRGC, its investment arm the IRGC Cooperative Foundation, and its construction conglomerate Khatam al Anbiya are all unlikely to be sought out as business partners by Western firms. The IRGC-controlled Basij Cooperative Foundation, however, is not sanctioned. Of the

---

(http://new.tse.ir/Instrument.html?IRO1PNES0001); "Leasing Rayan Saipa – *Sahamdaran* (Shareholders)," *Tehran Stock Exchange*, accessed September 13, 2015. (http://new.tse.ir/Instrument.html?IRO1RSAP0001); "*Siman Behbahan* (Behbahan Cement) – *Sahamdaran* (Shareholders)," *Tehran Stock Exchange*, accessed September 13, 2015. (http://new.tse.ir/Instrument.html?IRO1SBHN0001).

[92] U.S. Department of Treasury, Press Center, Press Release, "Treasury Targets Iran's Islamic Revolutionary Guards Corps," February 10, 2010. (http://www.treasury.gov/press-center/press-releases/Pages/tg539.aspx)

[93] The four Khatam Al-Anbiya's subsidiaries are Fater Engineering Institute, Imensazen Consultant Engineers Institute (ICEI), Makin Institute, and Rahab Institute.

Dr. Emanuele Ottolenghi   September 17, 2015

hundreds of companies controlled by Khatam Al-Anbiya and the two cooperative foundations, only a handful were ever identified and designated.

The gap between designated IRGC companies and those that have eluded U.S. or EU sanctions is wide, creating a window for the latter to now participate in the JCPOA economic windfall.

Over the years, Treasury has listed 19 individuals, 23 companies (not including the National Iran Oil Company and its subsidiaries), four military entities (the IRGC, its air force, its missile command, and its Quds Force), and two academic institutions. Additional listings have targeted companies, such as Iran Air, for providing logistical and financial support to the IRGC. The State Department has also sanctioned companies that belong to the IRGC, although not always as IRGC subsidiaries, such as the aforementioned Ofogh Saberin. The EU, for its part, has listed 25 companies as IRGC-owned or controlled commercial entities.

The list is far from exhaustive. Treasury's list was last updated on November 23, 2012. Since then, there have been no new IRGC designations, including against individuals, despite personnel changes that have occurred over the years. Brigadier General Rostam Qasemi, for example, was sanctioned in 2010 while he was commander of Khatam Al-Anbiya. In 2011, however, he became minister of petroleum. In March 2013, Brigadier General Ebadollah Abdollahi was appointed to replace him as commander of Khatem Al-Anbiya.[94] Since taking on this position, he has not been listed.

Proponents of the Iran deal may argue that this gap existed before the lifting of sanctions, and yet Iran's economy was weakened all the same. There is an important difference: under the sanctions regime, Iranian companies were blocked from accessing the global financial system, faced steep costs for transport and insurance, and had to accept systematic screening of their merchandise. Under the JCPOA, these barriers will no longer exist.

IRGC Companies that were never sanctioned

Tidewater Middle East PLC is an instructive example of how the current sanctions structure is insufficient to prevent the IRGC and its businesses from fully participating in the post-sanctions economic environment. Treasury designated Tidewater Middle East PLC on June 23, 2011[95] as an entity owned by the IRGC. The EU followed suit in January 2012.

Tidewater (not to be confused with the New Orleans-based Tidewater, Inc.) is Iran's largest port operator. According to Treasury, "Tidewater-managed ports are a crucial component of Iran's

[94] "New Commander of Khatam al-Anbiya," *Iran Daily Briefing*, March 5, 2013. (http://www.irandailybrief.com/2013/03/05/new-commander-of-khatam-al-anbia/)
[95] U.S. Department of Treasury, Press Release, "Fact Sheet: Treasury Sanctions Major Iranian Commercial Entities," June 23, 2011. (http://www.treasury.gov/press-center/press-releases/Pages/tg1217.aspx)

Dr. Emanuele Ottolenghi   September 17, 2015

infrastructure and transport network, and shipments into Tidewater facilities provide an avenue of revenue to the IRGC in support of its illicit conduct."[96]

Tidewater and its subsidiaries played a critical role in providing services to the IRGC and Iran's weapons shipments to Hamas and Hezbollah, some of which were interdicted in international waters. In all known cases, weapons cargoes disguised as commercial goods originated from the Bandar Abbas container terminal, which Tidewater manages. Tidewater was therefore an accomplice to illicit weapons transfers to support terrorism against U.S. allies.

Tidewater wholly owns (or controls a majority of shares of) a number of companies offering port services.[97] Despite their subsidiary relation to an entity sanctioned both by the U.S. and EU, none of them were designated. Two – Meyar Saham and Eftekhar Saham – are financial institutions involved in managing investments for their parent company. The lifting of general sanctions against Iran's financial sector will enable these IRGC affiliates to elude restrictions against the Guard and open investment portfolios overseas. The same principle extends to Tidewater's corporate management.[98]

IRGC Commanders who Eluded Sanctions

Many of the individuals mentioned in this testimony are not under U.S., UN, or EU sanctions today. While the U.S. retains authority to sanction them, the EU will not be in a position to do so, given that it cannot now impose new nuclear sanctions against delisted individuals.

As for the individuals who remain under U.S. or EU sanctions, in many cases the companies they manage have eluded sanctions. Masoud Mehrdadi is one key figure in the IRGC financial realm.[99] Mehrdadi's executive board membership encompasses a wide range of sectors, from

---

[96] U.S. Department of Treasury, Press Release, "Fact Sheet: Treasury Sanctions Major Iranian Commercial Entities," June 23, 2011. (http://www.treasury.gov/press-center/press-releases/Pages/tg1217.aspx)

[97] Tidewater subsidiaries are: Rahyab Rayaneh Gostar Company (RRGC); Sea Port Line Co. (Daryabandar Line Marine and Shipping Services Company); Negin Sabz Middle East Company (NSMEC); Sahel va Farasahel (Onshore & Offshore) Technology Training Company, Ltd; Persian Gulf Kish Line Marine Services Company; Darya Gostar Kish Company (DGKC); Meyar Saham Stock Market Agency; and Eftekhar Saham Investment Company (ESIC).

[98] The company's chairman Seyed Mehdi Motevalian and its board members were never designated. This includes Vice Chairman, Mehdi Etesam, who used to be the managing director of Sadra, another IRGC company under U.S. sanctions. Etesam represents the Commercial Services Ayande Negar Mehr Company, another IRGC firm not under sanctions. The current composition of the board is available on the company's website: "*Entekhab Ehsaye Jadid Hoyat Madireh-ye Sherkat-e Tidewater* (Select New Members of the Tidewater Board of Directors)," *Tidewater Company Website*, accessed September 13, 2015.
(http://www.tidewater.ir/Persian/News/Pr_NewsShow.aspx?NewsID=1927). Etesam was identified as the Sadra managing director in media coverage of Iran: Yeganeh Torbati & Jonathan Saul, "Iran launches its first home-built tanker," *Reuters*, July 24, 2012. (http://www.reuters.com/article/2012/07/24/us-iran-tanker-idUSBRE86N0NW20120724). Treasury sanctioned Sadra, designating it as a subsidiary of Khatam al-Anbiya, on March 28, 2012. U.S. Department of Treasury, Press Release, "Treasury Announces Additional Sanctions Against Iranian Engineering and Shipping Firms," March 28, 2012.
(http://www.treasury.gov/press-center/press-releases/Pages/tg1509.aspx)

[99] Little information is available on his service in the IRGC during the Iran-Iraq War, though he has been named among the ranks of senior prominent commanders including IRGC commander Mohammad Ali Jafari and Quds

energy to telecommunication to banking. He now sits on the executive board of the Guard's primary financial investor, the IRGC Cooperative Foundation, and its affiliated Ansar Bank.[100] Both have been designated by the U.S. as providers of financial services to the IRGC under Executive Order 13382 and by the EU under Regulation No 961/2010.[101] From 2012-2014, he was also a board member of the aforementioned Bahman Group.[102]

Gholamreza Jalali Farahani is another example. He chaired the board of three companies on behalf of the IRGC Cooperative Foundation. He currently also serves as head of Iran's Passive Defense Organization and previously was head of the IRGC's engineering department.[103] The Deputy Commander of the IRGC Ground Forces, Asghar Sabouri, also sat on the IRGC Cooperative Foundation's board.[104]

Mehrdadi, Farahani, and Sabouri are not under sanctions. They will enjoy, along with the companies they manage or managed on behalf of the IRGC, the full measure of rewards from the JCPOA unless U.S. authorities move to designate them.

There are other inconsistencies that the U.S. Treasury should address. Ahmad Vahid Dastjerdi, for example, is under sanctions for his role in Iran's ballistic missile program, but the companies he chairs are not. Dastjerdi is a veteran IRGC member and the current CEO of the IRGC Cooperative Foundation. Dastjerdi held three chairmanships on behalf the IRGC Cooperative

Force chief Qassem Soleimani. See Youhanna Najdi & Saeed Ghasseminejad, "*Pasdar Masoud Mehrdadi; Maghz-e Motefakker-e Emperatouri-ye Eghtesadi-ye Sepah* (Guard Masoud Mehrdadi; Mastermind of IRGC Economic Empire)," *Bamdad Khabar* (Iran), November 6, 2014. (http://bamdadkhabar.com/2014/11/33068/)

[100] Youhanna Najdi & Saeed Ghasseminejad, "*Pasdar Masoud Mehrdadi; Maghz-e Motefakker-e Emperatouri-ye Eghtesadi-ye Sepah* (Guard Masoud Mehrdadi; Mastermind of IRGC Economic Empire)," *Bamdad Khabar* (Iran), November 6, 2014. (http://bamdadkhabar.com/2014/11/33068/); Emanuele Ottolenghi & Saeed Ghasseminejad, "If the U.S. Wants a Nuclear Deal, It Needs to Fully Enforce Its Sanctions Against Iran's Revolutionary Guards," *Business Insider*, September 14, 2014. (http://www.businessinsider.com/sanctioning-the-irgc-is-the-path-to-a-nuclear-deal-2014-9)

[101] U.S. Department of Treasury, Press Release, "Fact Sheet: Treasury Designated Iranian Entities Tied to the IRGC and IRISL," August 21, 2010. (http://www.treasury.gov/press-center/press-releases/Pages/tg1010.aspx); Official Journal of the European Union, "Council Implementing Regulation (EU) No 503/2011 of 23 May 2011 Implementing Regulation (EU) No 961/2010 on Restrictive Measures Against Iran," October 25, 2010. (http://eur-lex.europa.eu/legal-content/EN/TXT/?uri=CELEX:32011R0503)

[102] Iran Securities and Exchange Organization, Bulletin, "*Tasmimat-e Majmae Omoumi-e Sherkat-e Gorouh-e Bahman* (Bahman Group General Assembly Decisions)," January 16, 2013. (http://www.codal.ir/Reports/BoardMemberChange.aspx?LetterSerial=ra2dm0ozeMy58dHj944klg%3D%3D); Iran Securities and Exchange Organization, Bulletin, "*Tasmimat-e Majmae Omoumi-e Sherkat-e Gorouh-e Bahman* (Bahman Group General Assembly Decisions)," June 29, 2013. (http://www.codal.ir/Reports/Assembly.aspx?LetterSerial=CCtdx8hOQOpzomXS7ZyTVA==)

[103] The three companies are Behsaz Bana Gostar Co., Fajr Qods Co., and Design and Idea Architecture Consultant Engineering Co. "Brigadier General Gholam Reza Jalali Farahani" *Iran Briefing*, January 28, 2012. (http://iranbriefing.net/brigadier-general-gholam-reza-jalali-farahani/)

[104] Sabouri served as a board member of the Foundation's auditing firm and of Misagh Basirat Institute,the Chairman of Alaleh Kabood Kavir Company, the Vice Chairman of Bama Company, the Chairman of the Veterans Housing Institute (Jahad-e-Khanesazi –e- Razmandegan), the Chairman of Laleh Welfare Service Company (Khadamat Refahi Laleh), the Vice Chairman of Tose'e Ma'aden Pahneh Tehran, and the Chairman of Triko Setareh Shargh, all on behalf of the IRGC Cooperative Foundation.

Foundation.[105] Although he himself is slated to remain indefinitely under U.S. sanctions and under EU sanctions until Transition Day, the companies he has managed are not.

Finally, there are commanders and executives who no longer officially work for the Guard but have set up their own consulting or construction companies. In many such instances these individuals may act as proxies for the IRGC. In the case of Gholam Hossein Khadjeali, for example, he was the CEO of the sanctioned Khatam al-Anbiya subsidiary Sepanir Oil and Gas Development Co. from 2007 to 2013 and since then has become the owner of a private energy contractor.[106].

The failure to sanction numerous senior IRGC executives and commanders means their ability to conduct business abroad on their companies' behalf will now be greatly enhanced.

Conclusions

In light of the above evidence, I draw the following conclusions:

- First, the evidence strongly suggests that the IRGC will greatly benefit financially, and therefore, by extension, politically, from the economic dividends generated by the JCPOA.

- Second, although technically sanctions against the IRGC remain in place in both Europe and the United States, the sanctions architecture that inflicted economic pain on the IRGC financial empire has largely eroded and the IRGC can easily circumvent the remaining provisions.

- Third, more legal steps are required to reconstitute effective tools to counter the IRGC, limit its ability to take advantage of the new economic climate, reduce its access to revenue and finance, and constrain the freedom of action of its leaders.

---

[105] He served as chairman of Paivaran Energy Development Co. (Toseye Energy Paivaran), the Basij Cooperative Foundation and Alaleh Kabood Kavir Co.

[106] Khadjeali's resume confirms more than a decade of continuous involvement as a senior IRGC executive. An engineer by training, Khadjeali still teaches at the U.S.-sanctioned, IRGC-controlled Imam Hossein University, where he lectures on tunnel construction. From 1995 to 2013 he continuously held executive positions in Khatam al-Anbiya subsidiaries, including managing director for Sepasad Engineering from 2005 to 2007. "Personnel Detail – Gholamhossein Khadjehali Chaleshtari (GH. Khadjehali)" *Iran Management Consultants Association Website*, accessed September 13, 2015.
(http://imc.org.ir/fa/?option=com_mtree&task=att_download&link_id=2648&cf_id=62). Khadjeali took leave of Khatam al-Anbiya in 2013 to launch his own energy consulting company, Mahdas Iranian Co. "Homepage" *Mahdas Iranian Company Website*, accessed September 8, 2015. (http://mahdas.com/). Within two years of its establishment, Mahdas Iranian had secured an important consultancy contract from the state-owned PEDEC for the North Yaran oilfield development project, and one for Mokran Petrochemical hub, the largest petrochemical complex in Iran, at Chabahar Free Zone. "North Yaran Oil Field Development," *Mahdas Iranian Company Website*, accessed September 13, 2015. (http://mahdas.com/core-and-pvt-analysis/) and "Mokran Petrochemical Complex," *Mahdas Iranian Company Website*, accessed September 13, 2015. (http://mahdas.com/mokran-petrochemical-complex/)

Recommendations

Therefore, I offer the following recommendations:

Congress should initiate legislation that would require the State Department to designate the IRGC as a Foreign Terrorist Organization (FTO):

The U.S. Department of State maintains a list of Foreign Terrorist Organizations that pose a threat to U.S. nationals and U.S. national security. There is little doubt that the IRGC has engaged in terrorist activity against U.S. nationals and threatened the national security of the United States. The U.S. Treasury Department has designated the IRGC Quds Force for its involvement in terrorism, but the State Department has not taken reciprocal actions. More broadly, the Quds Force is part of the IRGC. If the Quds Force is responsible for terrorism (as the U.S. government has indicated), then the IRGC as a whole should be designated as a terrorist organization and included on the FTO list.

Designating the IRGC will provide another warning to foreign companies mulling business in Iran. Additionally, the move would help mitigate some of the benefits that the IRGC is set to receive as a result of the JCPOA. Indeed, placing the IRGC on the FTO list enables the United States to maintain more leverage over certain financial interactions in which the IRGC is likely to attempt to engage.

Pushing for the inclusion of the IRGC on the FTO list is a way for members of Congress—both those who supported and those who opposed the JCPOA—to ensure that the JCPOA does not enable greater Iranian regional aggression.

For the IRGC to be removed from the FTO list, the organization would have to demonstrate that it no longer supports global terrorism or backs proxies such as Hezbollah, the Houthis in Yemen, and the Assad regime in Syria. To be removed from the list the IRGC would need to demonstrate a commitment to stability throughout the region.

As part of that legislation, Congress should declare that it is the policy of the United States that the IRGC is one organization responsible for all of the activities of its subsidiaries and branches:

Hezbollah is legally regarded in some European countries as having two separate parts: a military arm and a non-military arm. This makes it illegal to deal with the "military wing" of Hezbollah but not with other parts of the organization. Similarly, the U.S. government has determined that a branch of the IRGC, the Quds Force, is responsible for terrorism but the organization as a whole is not. Congress should declare in "Sense of Congress" language that any transaction with a part of the IRGC is the same as transacting with the Quds Force. Similarly, any activity by the Quds Force will be attributed to the IRGC as a whole.

There is a strong precedent for this. The U.S. has included Hezbollah and Hamas on the FTO list and argued that neither has a distinct "political wing" and "military wing," recognizing that the money is fungible, the branches are intertwined, and the leadership is the same. Congress now has an opportunity to state with clarity that this is also the case with the IRGC, the Quds Force, IRGC corporate holdings, and the smuggling networks, through which the IRGC has procured nuclear technology, facilitated human rights abuses within Iran, materially supported the Assad regime and Shiite militias in Iraq, and exported terrorism.

Congress can use future trade agreements with Europe to limit the IRGC's ability to operate in Europe:

The terms of the JCPOA require the EU and UN to delist many Iranian entities and lift sanctions against them. This includes both individuals associated with the IRGC and companies and foundations that have previously acted as pass-throughs for the IRGC to acquire financing, weapons, nuclear components, and transportation for troops and ammunition to foreign battlefields. Because of these de-listings, the IRGC will soon have a free hand in many European markets to purchase products and travel openly. The U.S. however has leverage over how open those markets will become to the IRGC.

The Transatlantic Trade and Investment Partnership between the U.S. and the EU is still being negotiated and the U.S. Trade Representative (USTR) maintains significant leverage over the terms. Congress could demand that the USTR require greater reporting on IRGC investments throughout Europe. The terms of the agreements could require that any country within the EU that is contracting with Iran certify that none of the entities are associated, in part or in whole, with the IRGC. The USTR could also require the EU to report annually on European companies investing in Iran, and therefore place those commercial transactions under public scrutiny. This may have a chilling effect because companies would be publicly associated with Iran and may suffer reputation damage as a result of business ties with the leading state sponsor of terrorism.

The administration should significantly increase the number of designations of both individuals and companies affiliated with, controlled, or owned by the IRGC:

Despite the optimism of some within the international business community over the JCPOA, businesses and the legal community still largely view Iran as a market and counter-party risk. The U.S., through designations and other policies, has played a significant role in this regard. Thus, if Congress and Treasury were to designate hundreds of IRGC companies before Implementation Day, this would send a clear warning not to rush into contracts with Iran. The message would be: IRGC companies are more numerous than you may think. A company with IRGC connections that is not yet on the SDN list today might be there tomorrow. In short, companies would take seriously the task of "know your business partner" before signing any contracts in Iran.

Congress should require Treasury to lower the ownership threshold for designation as an IRGC-owned entity:

The administration has stated that it will continue to enforce and enhance sanctions against Iran's illicit activities. Presumably this includes the IRGC. But the bureaucratic process of compiling a designation package can take months. Even the threshold for designation is often too high.

Congress should consider legislation that would help Treasury lower the threshold for identifying and designating a company as "owned or controlled by the IRGC" from 50+1% to 20% to better reflect the role IRGC plays in these companies. As noted above, the IRGC has engaged in a pattern of obfuscation to hide its control of many corporations. Additionally, even with a minority share, the IRGC often controls the board of directors. Accordingly, IRGC board membership might become part of the new criteria for Treasury designations.

Congress should require Treasury to create an IRGC Watch List:

Even when the threshold for designation is lowered, the IRGC is likely to engage in sanctions evasion and deceptive business practice to obscure its control. To address this problem, Congress can mandate that the U.S. Treasury maintain and publish an IRGC "watch list" which would report companies that do not reach the threshold for designation but have IRGC involvement. The list would serve as an aid to international companies considering transactions with Iranian companies. This list would signal to companies that if they are considering a business relationship with an entity on the IRGC watch list, their business partner is under scrutiny and might one day be designated.

Congress should encourage international corporations to demand an exclusion clause for ending commercial activities with designated or suspected IRGC entities:

As foreign companies re-enter the Iranian market, they are likely to unknowingly enter into business and financial transactions with Iranian entities owned or controlled by the IRGC. Congress, the U.S. Treasury, and their European counterparts could find ways to encourage companies investing in Iran to require their counterparts to certify that they are not wholly or in-part owned or operated by the IRGC. This could also include a declaration that shareholders do not include members of the IRGC. For companies requiring a license from Treasury's Office of Foreign Assets Control, this certification could be included in the licensing process.

Congress should also look into ways to provide protection such that if a company discovers that it is engaging in commercial activity with an entity that to its previous knowledge was not affiliated with the IRGC, that company would have the option of nullifying its contract. The aforementioned watch list could help to prevent such discoveries. But such protection would help further mitigate risk.

Closing remarks

Mr. Chairman, these recommendations may sound very ambitious, but a more aggressive approach to countering the IRGC is crucial. The IRGC is the crucible to the illicit conduct of the Iranian regime. The steps that I have proposed here could go a long way toward countering the Guards' aggressive conduct worldwide.

Thank you for the opportunity to testify today. I look forward to your questions.

NOTE: Appendices to the above prepared statement may be found on the Internet at http://docs.house.gov/Committee/Calendar/ByEvent.aspx?EventID=103958

Ms. Ros-Lehtinen. Thank you very much for those recommendations, Doctor.

Dr. Levitt?

STATEMENT OF MATTHEW LEVITT, PH.D., FROMER-WEXLER FELLOW, DIRECTOR, STEIN PROGRAM ON COUNTERTERRORISM AND INTELLIGENCE, WASHINGTON INSTITUTE FOR NEAR EAST POLICY

Mr. Levitt. Chairman Ros-Lehtinen, Ranking Member Deutch, members of the committee, thank you for the opportunity to appear before you today to discuss the recent activities of two of the major beneficiaries of the Iran deal: The IRGC and Lebanese Hezbollah.

Allow me to focus on Hezbollah.

Iran is Hezbollah's primary benefactor, giving the Lebanese party and militant group some $200 million a year, in addition to weapons training, intelligence, and logistical assistance. But over the past 18-plus months, Iran had cut back its financial support to Hezbollah, a collateral benefit of the unprecedented international sanctions regime targeting Iran's nuclear program as well as the fall in oil prices.

The cutback mostly curtailed Hezbollah's political, social, and military activities inside Lebanon. Its social service institutions cut costs. Employees received paychecks late or were laid off. Funding for organizations like its satellite television station Al Manar were reduced.

By contrast, Hezbollah's Syrian operations, which have been a priority for Tehran given its commitment to defending the regime of Bashar al-Assad, have shown no sign of financial hardship. In fact, Hezbollah is busier than ever, especially in Syria, where it is engaged in expensive militant operations and support activities.

Meanwhile, the group has expanded its regional activities further afield, straining its coffers, even as it had to cut back on its activities in Lebanon. With renewed funding from Iran, even a little bit of funding, Hezbollah would be more aggressive at home and abroad, challenging less militant parties across the Lebanese political spectrum and boosting its destabilizing activities outside of Lebanon.

The war in Syria has dramatically changed Hezbollah. The group is now a regional player engaged in conflicts far beyond its historic area of operations. The strongest indicators of Hezbollah's transformation are structural. Since 2013, it has added two new commands, one along the Lebanese-Syrian border and one in Syria itself, to its existing bases in Southern and Eastern Lebanon.

This points to a serious commitment to conflicts well beyond Lebanon's border. Today, there are between 6,000 and 8,000 Hezbollah operatives in Syria. Meanwhile, Hezbollah has transferred key personnel from its traditionally paramount southern command to Syria and even to Iraq and to Yemen.

Hezbollah's transformation into a regional actor is acutely felt by the group's operatives themselves. ''We should not be called Party of God,'' one Hezbollah commander told the Financial Times. ''We are not a party now. We are international. We are in Syria, we are in Palestine, we are in Iraq, and we are in Yemen. We are wherever the oppressed need us. Hezbollah is the school where every freedom-seeking man wants to learn.''

Meanwhile, Hezbollah remains committed to conducting terrorist activities around the world. And just about a year ago last September, the National Counterterrorism Center warned they remain concerned the group's activities could either endanger or target U.S. and other Western interests, not just Israel.

In April 2014, there was a Hezbollah operative arrested in Thailand; in November 2014, another in Peru, and this man had married an American citizen. Most recently, there was a new plot thwarted in Cyprus, where an individual who was a dual Lebanese-Canadian citizen had stockpiled 8.2 tons of ammonium nitrate. And, according to Israeli investigators, Hezbollah was using Cyprus as a point of export from which to funnel explosives for a series of attacks not just in Cyprus but elsewhere in Europe.

It is against this backdrop that sanctions relief will take place. And whatever amount of money Iran receives, it will presumably spend the bulk of these moneys on pressing domestic needs, but it will undoubtedly also direct substantial funding to foreign adventures. And that is something that none of us can tolerate. Even a small percentage of the lower-end estimates of Iran's sanctions relief would provide a windfall to its proxies.

In all likelihood, Iranian support for such behaviors will only increase in the wake of a deal. Iranian leaders who backed the deal will likely feel the need to prove their anti-American and pro-revolutionary bona fides, especially since the deal is widely seen in Iran as a victory for Rouhani and his allies over the IRGC and hardliners.

It is important to note, also, that we are losing at least one critical tool to combat Hezbollah's financing. In March 2014, then-Treasury Under Secretary David Cohen touted the collateral counterterrorism benefit of counterproliferation sanctions targeting Iran's banking and oil sections. He said, and I quote:

''In fact, the success of our unprecedented Iran sanctions regime, including sanctions on Iranian financial institutions and Iran's ability to sell its oil, has had the collateral benefit of squeezing Tehran's ability to fund terrorist groups such as Hezbollah.''

That will no longer be the case even as Iran remains, in the words of the Financial Action Task Force, an ongoing and substantial money-laundering and terror-financing risk.

A few weeks ago, a Saudi Hezbollah operative, Ahmed al-Mughassil, was detained in Lebanon. He was the mastermind of the 1996 Khobar Towers bombing. Hopefully, this is going to lead to a whole lot more intelligence-sharing between us and our Gulf allies. It should reveal a tremendous amount of information about Hezbollah, Lebanese Hezbollah, Saudi Hezbollah's connections to the IRGC.

One area of inquiry and action that could yield particularly positive results would be to target in fairly quick suggestion a variety of Hezbollah front companies and logistics nodes around the world. The theme of my written testimony is that Hezbollah relies heavily on such fronts to carry out its operations from Europe to Iraq, from China to Dubai.

But that can't be all we do. As Emanuele said, we need to also designate IRGC and Quds Force elements, as well, or the Iranians will feel that all we are doing is targeting their other proxies.

There are many areas of the Iran deal that warrant close attention as the deal moves toward implementation. Contending with what Secretary of the Treasury Jack Lew referred to as ''Iran's menacing behavior,'' in particular through the Quds Force and Hezbollah, must be at the top of the list. Failure to do so would not only undermine the logic of the Iran deal as articulated by the administration, it would add to the very real trust deficit currently affecting our relationships with allies both in the region and around the globe.

Thank you very much.

[The prepared statement of Mr. Levitt follows:]

Major Beneficiaries of the Iran Deal: IRGC and Hezbollah

Dr. Matthew Levitt

Fromer-Wexler Fellow and Director, Stein Program on Counterterrorism and Intelligence,
The Washington Institute for Near East Policy

Testimony submitted to the House Foreign Affairs Subcommittee on the Middle East and North Africa

September 17, 2015

Chairman Ileana Ros-Lehtinen, Ranking Member Deutch, and Members of the Committee, thank you for this opportunity to appear before you today to discuss the recent activities of two of the major beneficiaries of the Iran deal: Iran's Islamic Revolutionary Guard Corp (IRGC) and Lebanese Hezbollah, Iran's primary proxy active both as a regional militia and international terrorist group. Allow me to focus on Hezbollah.

Iran is Hezbollah's primary benefactor, giving the Lebanese political party and militant group some $200 million a year in addition to weapons, training, intelligence, and logistical assistance. Over the past eighteen months, however, Iran has cut back its financial support to Hezbollah -- a collateral benefit of the unprecedented international sanctions regime targeting Iran's nuclear program, as well as the fall in oil prices. The cutback has mostly curtailed Hezbollah's political, social, and military activities inside Lebanon. Its social-service institutions have cut costs, employees have received paychecks late or been laid off, and funding for civilian organizations, such as the group's satellite television station, al-Manar, has been reduced. By contrast, Hezbollah's Syria command, which has been a priority for Tehran given its commitment to defending Bashar al-Assad's regime, has shown no sign of financial hardship.

As a result of the sanctions relief due Tehran under the Iran deal, Hezbollah expects additional funds will come its way, which will enable Hezbollah to push back against Lebanese political and social movements that are uncomfortable with its intervention in Syria. Lebanon's political crises, from its inability to select a president to its failure to collect garbage, are a result of this deep sectarian division. An influx of radicalized Sunnis from Syria is already setting the stage for still further instability in Lebanon.

Increased Iranian spending will also benefit Hezbollah's regional and international operations. The group is no longer limited to jockeying for political power in Lebanon and fighting Israel. With more money, it could step up its aid to Shia militias in Iraq and Yemen in cooperation with Iran, sending small numbers of skilled trainers to bolster local forces and, in some cases, fight alongside them. In Iraq, Hezbollah is training and fighting with Shia militias. Though they are fighting on behalf of the government, their tactics exacerbate sectarian tensions. Its footprint in Yemen is small, but it could expand with additional resources. Hezbollah is already trying to find long-term support for these operations. In Iraq, for example, it is investing in commercial front organizations.

Finally, increased funding could help Hezbollah reconstitute its capabilities beyond the Middle East. The group has expanded its terrorist operations in countries as disparate as Cyprus, Peru, and Thailand.

Hezbollah is busier than ever, especially in Syria, where it is engaged in expensive militant operations and support activities. Meanwhile, the group has expanded its regional activities further afield, straining its coffers even as it has had to cut back its activities in Lebanon. A newly enriched Hezbollah would be more aggressive at home and abroad, challenging less-militant parties across the Lebanese political spectrum and boosting its destabilizing activities outside of Lebanon.

Hezbollah's War in Syria

The war in Syria has dramatically changed Hezbollah. Once limited to jockeying for political power in Lebanon and fighting Israel, the group is now a regional player engaged in conflicts far beyond its historic area of operations, often in cooperation with Iran. Underscoring this strategic shift, Hezbollah has transferred key personnel previously stationed near the Israel-Lebanon border to a newly established Syrian command and to outposts even further abroad, in Iraq and Yemen.

Initially, Hezbollah Secretary-General Hassan Nasrallah resisted dispatching his fighters to Syria to back President Bashar al-Assad, despite repeated requests from Iranian leaders, in particular Qods Force commander Qassem Soleimani. Like some other Hezbollah leaders, Nasrallah feared that engaging in Syria would undermine Hezbollah's position in Lebanon by associating Hezbollah—Lebanon's primary Shiite party—with a repressive Iranian-allied government butchering a Sunni-majority population. But Nasrallah reportedly acquiesced after receiving an appeal from Iranian Supreme Leader Ayatollah Ali Khamenei. Iran, Khamenei made clear, expected Hezbollah to support Assad's grip on power. This operational shift has transformed Hezbollah from a Lebanese party focused on domestic politics into regional sectarian force acting at Iran's behest across the Middle East.

The strongest indicators of Hezbollah's transformation are structural. Since 2013, Hezbollah has added two new commands—the first on the Lebanese-Syrian border, the second within Syria itself—to its existing bases in southern and eastern Lebanon. This startling reorganization points to a serious commitment to civil conflicts well beyond Lebanon's borders. Today, there are between some 6,000 and 8,000 Hezbollah operatives in Syria.

In establishing its new presence in Syria, Hezbollah has transferred key personnel from its traditionally paramount Southern Command, along Lebanon's border with Israel. Mustafa Badreddine, the head of Hezbollah's foreign terrorist operations, began coordinating Hezbollah military activities in Syria in 2012 and now heads the group's Syrian command. Badreddine is a Hezbollah veteran implicated in the 1983 bombing of U.S. barracks in Beirut, the 2005 assassination of former Lebanese Prime Minister Rafik Hariri, and terrorist bombings in Kuwait, among other attacks. His appointment is the strongest sign Hezbollah can give of its commitment to Syria's civil war. Other personnel assignments include Abu Ali Tabtabai, a long-time Hezbollah commander. He was transferred from a position in southern Lebanon to Hezbollah's Syria command, where he served as one of Badreddine's senior officers, overseeing many of the highly trained troops formerly under his control in Lebanon. Hezbollah's focus on the Syrian conflict extends to the top of the organization as well: Nasrallah has directed the group's activities in Syria since at least September 2011, when he reportedly began meeting Assad in Damascus to coordinate Hezbollah's contributions to the country's civil war. Indeed, the organization's intense focus on the Syrian conflict was the main reason for its redesignation by the U.S. Department of the Treasury in 2012.

But joining the fight in Syria did not come without risk. Hezbollah has suffered some serious personnel losses as a result, both in Lebanon and in Syria. Hassan al-Laqis, Hezbollah's chief military procurement officer, was assassinated in Beirut in December 2013; although the prime suspects were Israeli agents, Sunni extremists retaliating for Hezbollah's support for the Assad government have not been ruled out. And numerous high-ranking officers, including Fawzi Ayub, a longtime member of Hezbollah's foreign terrorist wing, have reportedly been killed in Syria in clashes with anti-Assad rebels. By the first half of 2015, Hezbollah was suffering between 60 and 80 weekly casualties in Syria's Qalamoun region alone. The deaths of Hezbollah members of Ayub's stature in Syria—and the sheer number of militants killed and wounded there—demonstrate Hezbollah's seriousness in defending the Assad regime. Its tolerance for such losses, on the other hand, reveals that Hezbollah increasingly considers the Syrian conflict an existential fight—for its domestic standing in Lebanon, on the one hand, and for the position of Shiite forces in Syria's bitter sectarian conflict, on the other.

Hezbollah Operations in Iraq and Yemen

Even as it deepens its activities in Syria, Hezbollah continues to aid Shiite militias in Iraq, sending small numbers of skilled trainers to fight the Islamic State (also known as ISIS) and defend Shiite shrines there. According to the U.S. Department of the Treasury, Hezbollah has also invested in commercial front organizations to support its operations in Iraq. In June, Treasury designated Hezbollah member Adham Tabaja, the majority owner of the Lebanon-based real estate and construction firm Al-Inmaa Group for Tourism Works, and reported he has exploited the firm's Iraqi subsidiaries to fund Hezbollah, with the assistance of Kassem Hejeij, a Lebanese businessman tied to Hezbollah, and Husayn Ali Faour, a member of Hezbollah's overseas terrorism unit.

As in Iraq, Hezbollah has dispatched only a small number of highly skilled trainers and fighters to Yemen. But as in Syria, the prominence of the operatives that Hezbollah has sent there demonstrates the importance the group attributes to the country's ongoing civil conflict. Khalil Harb, a former special operations commander and a close adviser to Nasrallah, oversees Hezbollah's activities in Yemen, managing the transfer of funds to the organization within the country and travelling frequently to Tehran to coordinate Hezbollah activities with Iranian officials. Given his experience working with other terrorist organizations, his close relations with Iranian and Hezbollah leaders, and his expertise in special operations and training, appointing Harb to work in Yemen no doubt made a great deal of sense to Hezbollah. In May, Saudi Arabia sanctioned Harb and another Hezbollah operative, Muhammad Qabalan, for their involvement in the country's conflict.

Harb, however, would not be the most senior operative Hezbollah has dispatched to Yemen. In the spring of 2015, Hezbollah sent Abu Ali Tabtabai, the senior Hezbollah commander formerly stationed in Syria, to upgrade the group's training program for Yemen's Houthi rebels, which reportedly involves schooling them in guerilla tactics. "Sending in Tabtabai [to Yemen] is a sign of a major Hezbollah investment and commitment," an Israeli official told me. "The key question is how long someone of Tabtabai's stature will stay."

Hezbollah's Long-Term Commitment to Regional Adventurism

In Syria and elsewhere, deadly proxy conflicts—between Saudi Arabia and other Sunni Gulf states, on the one hand, and Iran on the other—have been complicated by the dangerous overlay of sectarianism. Sunni and Shiite states and their clients seem to view the region's wars as a part of a long-term, existential struggle between their sects. Indeed, the war in Syria is now being fought on two parallel fronts: one between the Assad regime and the Syrian opposition, and the other between Sunni and Shiite communities over the threat each perceives in the other. Similar dynamics define the wars in Iraq and Yemen. Factional conflict might be negotiable, but sectarian war is almost certainly not.

Hezbollah's involvement in the war in Syria may have originally focused on supporting the Assad regime, but it now considers that war an existential battle for the future of the region, and for Hezbollah's place in it. As a result, Hezbollah's regional focus will likely continue for the foreseeable future. Together with other Iranian-backed militias, the group will continue to head an emerging Shiite foreign legion working both to defend Shiite communities and to expand Iranian influence across the region.

Even as it juggles its involvement in the conflicts of Iraq, Syria, and Yemen, Hezbollah must also balance its occasionally clashing ideological and political goals elsewhere. Hezbollah's adherence to the Iranian doctrine of *velayat-e faqih*, (guardianship of the jurist), which holds that a Shiite cleric should serve as the supreme head of government, binds Hezbollah to the decrees of Iranian clerics. But this complicates Hezbollah's other commitments to the Lebanese state, Lebanon's Shiite community, and Shiites abroad, because the interests of Iranian and Lebanese leaders often diverge. Hezbollah has long navigated these conflicting obligations with skill, but it will become increasingly difficult to do so as the group's priorities take it further afield from Beirut. Indeed, Lebanon is deeply divided along confessional and sectarian lines, so when Hezbollah fights against Sunnis abroad, it undermines its own ability to navigate domestic Lebanese politics.

Meanwhile, Hezbollah's intimate cooperation with Iran's Qods Force in Syria is drawing it still closer into Tehran's orbit, and thus deeper into the region's ongoing conflicts. By some accounts, Hezbollah units on the ground in Syria are sometimes instructed by the group's leadership to do one thing, but then once on the ground they are redirected by IRGC officials to do something else, and they are increasingly listening to the final word from the IRGC. In any event, Hezbollah's transformation is acutely felt by the group's operatives themselves. "We shouldn't be called Party of God," one Hezbollah commander told *The Financial Times* in May. "We're not a party now, we're international. We're in Syria, we're in Palestine, we're in Iraq and we're in Yemen. We are wherever the oppressed need us... Hezbollah is the school where every freedom-seeking man wants to learn."

Hezbollah Global Terrorist Operations Continue Apace

Three years ago this summer, Hezbollah blew up a bus of tourists in Bulgaria. The European Union then banned the military wing of Hezbollah. But despite both being blacklisted by Brussels and being heavily invested in the Syrian war, Hezbollah continues to plot attacks around the world, with a particular focus on Europe and South America.

"Beyond its role in Syria," Matt Olsen, the then-director of the National Counterterrorism Center (NCTC) warned in September 2014, "Lebanese Hezbollah remains committed to conducting terrorist activities worldwide." Nor are these plots only Israel's concern. The NCTC director continued: "We remain concerned the group's activities could either endanger or target U.S. and other Western interests." NCTC officials note that Hezbollah "has engaged in an aggressive terrorist campaign in recent years and continues attack planning abroad." Over the past few years Hezbollah plots either failed or were foiled as far afield as South Africa, Azerbaijan, India, Nigeria, Cyprus, Thailand, Turkey, and Bulgaria.

In April 2014, two Hezbollah operatives were arrested in Thailand, one of whom admitted that the two were there to carry out a bomb attack targeting Israeli tourists in Bangkok, according to U.S. counterterrorism officials. The plots underscored the threat posed by Hezbollah to civilian centers, the officials added. Authorities were also concerned that the operatives were Lebanese dual citizens, one a French national and the other Filipino.

More recently, Peruvian counterterrorism police arrested a Hezbollah operative in Lima in November 2014, the result of a surveillance operation that began several months earlier. In that case, Mohammed Amadar, a Lebanese citizen, arrived in Peru in November 2013 and married a dual Peruvian-American woman two weeks later. They soon moved to Brazil, living in Sao Paulo until they returned to Lima in July 2014. Authorities were clearly aware of Amadar at the time, because they questioned him on arrival at the airport and began watching him then. When he was arrested in October, police raided his home and found traces of TNT, detonators, and other inflammable substances. A search of the garbage outside his home found chemicals used to manufacture explosives. By the time of his arrest, intelligence indicated Amadar's targets included places associated with Israelis and Jews in Peru, including areas popular with Israeli backpackers, the Israeli embassy in Lima, and Jewish community institutions.

Hezbollah has long been active in South America, from the Tri-border Area where the borders of Argentina, Paraguay, and Brazil meet to Chile, Uruguay, and more. This trend continues, as the State Department noted in its annual terrorism report, where it highlighted the financial support networks Hezbollah maintains in places like Latin America and Africa. According to Brazilian police reports, Hezbollah helped a Brazilian prison gang, the First Capital Command (PCC), obtain weapons in exchange for protecting prisoners of Lebanese origin detained in Brazil. Lebanese traffickers tied to Hezbollah reportedly helped sell C4 explosives that the PCC allegedly stole in Paraguay. Moreover, the juxtaposition of Hezbollah plotting in Thailand and South America is nothing new: In 1994, Hezbollah nearly blew up the Israeli embassy in Bangkok just weeks before it successfully bombed the AMIA Jewish Community Center in Buenos Aires.

The latest plot was thwarted this summer in Cyprus, where Hussein Bassam Abdallah, a dual Lebanese-Canadian citizen, stockpiled 8.2 tons of ammonium nitrate, a popular chemical explosive. In July, Abdallah pled guilty to all eight charges against him -- including participation in a terrorist group (read: Hezbollah), possessing explosives, and conspiracy to commit a crime. It was the second time in three years that a Cypriot court has sentenced a Hezbollah operative to prison for plotting an attack in Cyprus. But this latest plot is different, in part because it reveals that the EU's warnings to Hezbollah not to operate on European soil have not dissuaded the group at all.

Back in July 2012, Cypriot authorities watched Hussam Yaacoub, a dual Lebanese-Swedish Hezbollah operative, conduct surveillance of Israeli tourists and arrested him in his hotel room a few hours later (he was ultimately convicted and jailed). A few days later, a group of Hezbollah operatives -- one of them a French citizen -- blew up a bus of Israeli tourists in Burgas, Bulgaria. Brussels was faced with the reality that Hezbollah was dispatching European operatives to carry out operations on European soil.

After months of often acrimonious deliberations, senior European officials gathered in Brussels in July 2013 to announce that all 28 EU member states agreed to add Hezbollah's military wing -- not the organization itself -- to the EU's list of banned terrorist groups. At the time, European officials pointed to the blacklisting as a shot across the bow. "This is a signal to terrorist organizations," German Foreign Minister Guido Westerwelle warned. "If you attack one of our European countries, you get an answer from all of them."

Fast forward two years. New evidence reveals that Hezbollah's military wing is still plotting attacks across Europe. We now know that the explosive material recently found in Cyprus was stored in the basement of a house in a residential Larnaca neighborhood sometime in 2011. In other words, these two Cyprus plots were not consecutive, but overlapping and possibly connected. By the time the EU banned Hezbollah's military wing, the recently seized explosives had already been in the country for over a year, maybe two. Hussein Abdallah made around ten trips to Cyprus to check on the explosives stockpile starting in 2012. He was paid handsomely to serve as guardian of chemicals: he was arrested carrying 9,400 euros, which he conceded was his latest payment from Hezbollah.

Abdallah admitted that Hezbollah planned to mount attacks in Cyprus targeting Israeli or Jewish interests there, but that was hardly the full scope of the operation. Indeed, the amount of explosives Hezbollah stockpiled would have facilitated many attacks. According to Israeli investigators, Hezbollah was using Cyprus as a "point of export" from which to funnel explosives elsewhere for a series of attacks in Europe. Indeed, the plot was already in motion: investigators believe the explosives used in the 2012 Burgas bus bombing may have come from the batch of chemicals stored in Cyprus.

The threat to Europe was real. Not only did Hezbollah actively maintain an explosives stockpile in Cyprus, the group retained the operatives, infrastructure and reach to engage in operations across Europe. Over the course of time Abdallah maintained this explosives stockpile, Hezbollah remained active across Europe, from a 2012 bombing thwarted in Greece to the arrest and deportation of a Hezbollah operative in Denmark in 2013 who arrived on a commercial ship for purposes still unknown. Four months after the EU ban, in late 2013, two Lebanese passengers at a Brussels airport were caught with nearly 770,000 euros in their possession. At least some of this cash was suspected to be intended for Hezbollah's coffers, Europol reported in a report earlier this year on the use of cash by criminal groups to launder money. A few months later, Germany raided the offices of the Orphan Children Project Lebanon in Essen, accusing the group of serving as a Hezbollah fundraising front organization. In its last annual report, Germany's domestic intelligence agency noted that Hezbollah maintains some 950 active operatives in the country.

Hezbollah weapons and technology procurement operations continued in Europe as well. In July 2014, the US Treasury blacklisted a Lebanese consumer electronics business, Stars Group Holding, along with its owners, subsidiaries, and "certain managers and individuals who support their illicit activities." Together, they functioned as a "key Hezbollah procurement network" that purchased technology around the world -- including in Europe -- to develop the drones Hezbollah deploys over Israel and Syria.

Abdallah's last assignment was to find a storage facility where the explosives stockpile could be stored, suggesting the plan to move small batches of the material to multiple locations across Europe may have been moving forward. While Abdallah traveled on his authentic Canadian passport, Hezbollah provided him a forged British identity card to use locally in Cyprus to rent the facility. This may have been his undoing, since traveling on authentic documents and using forgeries to conduct local, non-governmental business has become a preferred modus operandi for Hezbollah. Otherwise, authorities may not have picked up on the shipments themselves: Hezbollah reportedly is using commercial front companies under deep cover -- some as far away as China and Dubai -- to ship the dual-use chemicals it uses to manufacture explosives.

Some Money will Logically Flow to Bad Actors

According to the State Department's latest terrorist report, released in June, "Iran continued to sponsor terrorist groups around the world, principally through its Islamic Revolutionary Guard Corps-Qods Force (IRGC-QF)...These groups included Lebanese Hezbollah, several Iraqi Shia militant groups, Hamas, and Palestine Islamic Jihad." In addition, the State Department accused Iran of "prolonging the civil war in Syria, and worsening the human rights and refugee crisis there." The report described Iran's terror sponsorship as "undiminished." The report also described how Iran increased training and funding for its militias in 2014, supplying them with advanced weaponry. Iran also "provided hundreds of millions of dollars" to Hezbollah and "trained thousands of [the group's] fighters at camps in Iran." The State Department concluded that it does not expect Iran's behavior in Syria to change anytime soon, asserting that "Iran views Syria as a crucial causeway in its weapons supply route to [Hezbollah], its primary beneficiary, and as a key pillar in its 'resistance' front." Indeed, Iran continued to provide the group with "training, weapons, and explosives, as well as political, diplomatic, monetary, and organizational aid."

It is against this backdrop that Iran sanctions relief will take place. Whatever the amount of money Iran receives from sanctions relief—in congressional testimony in July Secretary Lew put the number around $50 billion, but the President himself referred in May to "$150 billion parked outside the country"—Iran will gain access to at least tens of billions of dollars, at first from blocked accounts and later from additional oil sales. And while administration officials have acknowledged that Iran engages in a wide range of nefarious activities, Treasury Secretary Jack Lew opined in April that "Most of the money Iran receives from sanctions relief will not be used to support those activities."

Presumably, Tehran will indeed spend the vast bulk of these monies on pressing domestic needs. But it will undoubtedly also direct substantial funding to foreign adventures, proxies and allies in keeping with its longstanding track record. That is indeed the expectation of Iran's allies in the region. Hezbollah Secretary General Hassan Nasrallah noted in April that even under sanctions Iran funded its allies, and anticipated that a now "rich and powerful Iran, which will be open to the world" would be able to do even more: "I say that in the next phase Iran will be able to stand by its allies, friends, the people in the region, and especially the resistance in Palestine and the Palestinian people more than any time in the past, and this is what the others are afraid of."

Even a small percentage of the lower end estimates of Iran's sanction relief windfall would enable Tehran to underwrite a significant increase in what Secretary Lew correctly referred to as "Iran's menacing behavior." In fact, in all likelihood Iranian support for such behaviors will only increase in the wake of a deal over Iran's nuclear program. Iranian leaders who backed the deal will likely feel the need to prove their anti-American and pro-revolutionary bona fides, especially since the deal is widely seen in Iran as a victory for Rouhani and his allies over the Islamic Revolutionary Guard Corp (IRGC) and other hardliners. The Supreme Leader himself may also feel the need—or it may simply be in his interest—to give the IRGC and the Qods Force greater latitude to behave aggressively in the region as a means of balancing domestic bases of power within Iran at a time when Rouhani would be riding high in the wake of the Iran deal.

Terrorism designations will not be removed under the Iran deal, including CISADA secondary sanctions—which is good. But in the past the Treasury Department pointed to the impact of WMD-proliferation sanctions on Hezbollah's bottom line, acknowledging the fungibility of funds across the spectrum of Iran's illicit financial conduct. In March 2014, then-Treasury Undersecretary David Cohen touted the collateral counterterrorism benefit of counter-proliferation sanctions targeting Iran's banking and oil sectors: "In fact, the success of our unprecedented Iran sanctions regime—including sanctions on Iranian financial institutions and

Iran's ability to sell its oil—has had the collateral benefit of squeezing Tehran's ability to fund terrorist groups such as Hezbollah." That will no longer be the case.

The administration says it intends to keep Iran's feet to the fire on these behaviors. "Make no mistake; deal or no deal, we will continue to use all our available tools, including sanctions, to counter Iran's menacing behavior," Treasury Secretary Jack Lew said in April. "Iran knows that our host of sanctions focused on its support for terrorism and its violations of human rights are not, and have never been, up for discussion. The Treasury Department's designations of Iranian-backed terrorist groups...will persist, giving us a powerful tool to go after Iran's attempts to fund terror." There is, however, a very real trust deficit between the administration and both the U.S. public and our allies in the region regarding U.S. policy toward the Middle East (think: chemical weapons red-line) and the Iran deal in particular (think: inspections anywhere, anytime). And here's the rub: to effectively counter Iran's menacing behaviors Iranian entities—banks, big business, bonyad foundations—will have to be potential targets for "all our available tools, including sanctions." But the text of the Iran deal itself enshrines Iran's own red-line on sanctions: "Iran has stated that if sanctions are reinstated in whole or in part, Iran will treat that as grounds to cease performing its commitments under the JCPOA in whole or in part." Will the U.S. risk undermining the Iran deal by sanctioning Iranian entities for supporting terrorism or abusing human rights?

The Risks That Remain

In June, the Financial Action Task Force (FATF) issued its latest public statement identifying jurisdictions with "strategic deficiencies" related to money laundering and terrorist financing which pose risks to the international financial system. As the technocratic, apolitical, multilateral body charged with setting global standards for anti-money laundering and counter-terror financing, FATF is uniquely positioned to opine on these matters. It is therefore very significant that FATF found that (as in past reports) only two jurisdictions—Iran and North Korea—present such "ongoing and substantial money laundering and terrorist financing (ML/TF) risks" that the international community should apply active "counter-measures" to protect themselves and the larger international financial system.

FATF's statement on Iran included this blunt language:

> The FATF remains particularly and exceptionally concerned about Iran's failure to address the risk of terrorist financing and the serious threat this poses to the integrity of the international financial system, despite Iran's recent engagement with the FATF.
>
> The FATF reaffirms its call on members and urges all jurisdictions to advise their financial institutions to give special attention to business relationships and transactions with Iran, including Iranian companies and financial institutions. In addition to enhanced scrutiny, the FATF reaffirms its 25 February 2009 call on its members and urges all jurisdictions to apply effective counter-measures to protect their financial sectors from money laundering and financing of terrorism (ML/FT) risks emanating from Iran. The FATF continues to urge jurisdictions to protect against correspondent relationships being used to bypass or evade counter-measures and risk mitigation practices and to take into account ML/FT risks when considering requests by Iranian financial institutions to open branches and subsidiaries in their jurisdiction. Due to the continuing terrorist financing threat emanating from Iran, jurisdictions should consider the steps already taken and possible additional safeguards or strengthen existing ones.

But now, under the Iran deal, most of the world, including Europe, will be looking to expand business relationships with Iran even as these "strategic deficiencies" related to Iran's money laundering and terror financing activities remain. And those deficiencies are nowhere as broad and blatant as they are in regards to the Islamic Republic's financial and material support to Hezbollah.

Conclusion

A few weeks ago, senior Saudi Hezbollah operative Ahmed al-Mughassil was detained in Lebanon and sent to Saudi Arabia where he has long been wanted on charges of masterminding and carrying out the 1996 Khobar Towers bombing. Mughassil has been an intimate and longtime confidante of the IRGC and Qods Force, working closely with both Iranian and Lebanese Hezbollah operatives. His arrest and interrogation should reveal still more details about the nature of the relationships between the IRGC and Qods Force on the one hand and Lebanese Hezbollah and its regional allies, especially in the Gulf, on the other. One can only hope that the timing of this arrest is the result of a renewed push to collect timely information about these group's activities for the purpose of taking tangible action against them.

One area of inquiry and action that could yield particularly positive results would be to target, in fairly quick succession, a variety of Hezbollah front companies and logistics nodes around the world. A theme woven throughout this testimony is that Hezbollah relies heavily on such front organizations to carry out its operations, from Europe to Iraq and from China to Dubai.

In July, the Treasury Department designated one such network, which was focused on supporting the group's activities in Syria. In July, Treasury described Abd al-Nur Shalan as "a businessman with close ties to Hezbollah leadership" who served as Hezbollah's "point person for the procurement and transshipment of weapons and materiel for the group and its Syrian partners for at least 15 years." Shalan, Treasury informed, "has been critical in keeping Hezbollah supplied with weapons, including small arms, since the start of the Syrian conflict." Shalan has been at the center of brokering business deals involving Hezbollah, including one for Syrian officials with companies in Belarus, Russia, and Ukraine regarding the purchase and sale of weapons. In 2010, he acquired a number of tons of anhydride, used in the production of explosives and narcotics, for use by Hezbollah.

Targeting Hezbollah's financial and logistical choke points is very effective, but only if done in a steady stream of actions, not a series of one-off designations from which Hezbollah can easily recover by rerouting its financing and logistics through other fronts.

Indeed, actions such as these will be all the more necessary now that Russian forces are reportedly on the ground in Syria. Israeli officials are not so much concerned that Russia will start arming Hezbollah directly, but that the Russian presence on the ground could mitigate Israel's ability to target Iranian arms shipments intended for Hezbollah as the Israeli air forces has done in the past.

While the Iran deal leaves much open to interpretation, one thing is certain: for Iran this deal is strictly transactional, not transformational. To the contrary, Iran is almost certain to increase its clandestine activities and support for proxies engaged in asymmetric warfare and reasonably deniable intelligence and terrorist operations. In other words, Hezbollah is about to take a place of even greater prominence within the planning of Iran's revolutionary elite. Hezbollah heeded Tehran's call to step into the breach of the Syrian war, and as a result has drifted even further into the Iranian orbit as a result of its intimate operations with the IRGC there.

But designating only Hezbollah entities—or those connected to other Shiite militia or terrorist groups answering to Iran—is not enough. Whether through Treasury designations or other tools, IRGC and Qods Force officers and entities engaged in Iran's ongoing illicit conduct must also be taken to task.

There are many areas of the Iran deal that warrant close attention as the deal moves toward implementation. Contending with what Secretary Lew referred to as "Iran's menacing behavior"—in particular through its own IRGC Qods Force and Lebanese Hezbollah—must be at the top of the list. Failure to do so would not only undermine the logic of the Iran deal as articulated by the administration, it would add to the very real trust deficit currently affecting our relationships with allies both in the region and around the globe.

Ms. Ros-Lehtinen. Thank you, Dr. Levitt. Dr. Maloney?

STATEMENT OF SUZANNE MALONEY, PH.D., INTERIM DEPUTY DIRECTOR, CENTER FOR MIDDLE EAST POLICY, THE BROOKINGS INSTITUTION

Ms. Maloney. Chair Ros-Lehtinen, Ranking Member Deutch, members of the committee, thank you so much for the opportunity to appear before the committee today on this very important issue.

The wide-ranging sanctions relief incorporated in the Iran nuclear deal has elicited what I believe to be a widely shared sense of affront at the appearance of rewarding Tehran after decades of bad behavior. And this is magnified by the irony that Washington is being forced to effectively cede the most effective instrument in its policy toolbox, the sanctions regime, at the very moment when its efficacy has finally been confirmed, even as some of the most strategically relevant aspects of the Iranian challenge remain unabated. That unescapable reality underscores the importance of identifying and implementing new mechanisms for addressing Iran's problematic regional policies.

Let me emphasize just two aspects of my written testimony. The first is the question of what Tehran will do with the money that it receives from the sanctions relief and the new trade and investment that is facilitated by the post-deal context.

The public discussion of the deal and its provisions have tended to emphasize the availability of new resources for Tehran's support of terrorist groups and other violent proxies, as well as its assiduous efforts to extend its influence across the region. However, it should be acknowledged that the most pressing needs facing Tehran today are not those related to its regional posture but to its domestic economy.

The sanctions regime that was so effective in succeeding in shifting Iran's approach and changing its longstanding nuclear recalcitrance did not come as a result of restrictions that impeded its ability to sustain its regional policies but, rather, because of the more immediate and potentially unsettling implications for the stability and the survival of the regime at home. The sanctions were felt far more immediately and more profoundly by the average Iranian than by the average beneficiary of Tehran's terror subsidies.

And it was these concerns about the erosion of Iran's economic base and the legitimacy of the system that generated the decision to negotiate in full seriousness and the elevation of Hassan Rouhani. For this reason, it is important to appreciate that the domestic requirements and priorities will loom large in the allocation of deal-related windfalls that will accrue to Tehran over the course of the next year. Rouhani is keenly concerned with Iran's dire economic predicament. Rehabilitation is ranked at the top of his agenda, in parallel with the nuclear file.

This isn't simply a matter of policy preferences for Rouhani and his team. Iran has real politics, and its population is impatient to reap the peace dividend that it was promised more than 2 years ago when they elected Rouhani to the Presidency with the expectation of an end to the nuclear impasse.

Let me also speak to the question of how sanctions relief will impact Iran's regional policies. Unfortunately, the long-term track record is clear: Iran's support for terrorism has never been driven primarily or even substantially by resource availability. In fact, Iran's most destructive regional policies have been undertaken and sustained at times of epic sanctions and economic constraints.

These policies were initiated during the early post-revolutionary period, just at the moment that Iran's economy reached its lowest point as a result of revolutionary chaos and upheaval and the eventual Iraqi invasion of Iran and throughout the long, brutal, and costly war that followed. In fact, many of Iran's worst regional abuses took place during this first decade, mentioned during the chair and the ranking member's statements: The cultivation of Hezbollah, the 1983 and 1984 bombings, and the direct and deadly assistance to subversive groups around the region.

The same trends have held course over the past decade as externally imposed economic pressures as well as the fall in oil prices have reached or even surpassed the heights of the hardships during the war. Sanctions have provided no remedy to Iran's efforts to extend its influence through nefarious activities and allies and its substantial investment in fueling and fighting conflicts in Iraq and Syria.

Even since 2010, as the world has targeted Iran's regional power projection and its support for terrorist proxies, there is little evidence that sanctions have impeded Iran's most destabilizing policies.

So the question that concerns the committee today is, what can we do? My colleagues have, I think, provided a number of important and constructive recommendations. Sanctions relief will undoubtedly exacerbate the challenges that we face, but the nuclear deal takes one of the most pressing aspects of the problem off the table at least for the next decade.

This provides us an opportunity to construct a bipartisan approach here at home and to, for the first time in the history of the Islamic Republic, really create a multilateral, durable alliance that addresses the regional challenge that Iran poses.

Thank you.

[The prepared statement of Ms. Maloney follows:]

Testimony of
Suzanne Maloney
Senior Fellow and Deputy Director of Foreign Policy
The Brookings Institution

Hearing: Major Beneficiaries of the Iran Deal: The IRGC and Hezbollah
Subcommittee on the Middle East and North Africa
Committee on Foreign Affairs, U.S. House of Representatives
September 17, 2015

Chairman Royce, Ranking Member Deutch, Members of the Committee, thank you for the invitation to appear before the Committee today. I am honored to appear before you today to discuss the impact of sanctions relief under the Joint Comprehensive Plan of Action, particularly with respect to Iran's regional influence and activities.

The JCPOA will entail enormous benefits for Iran's economy and, as a result, provide substantial additional resources available to the government of Iran. On "Implementation Day," which is anticipated to arrive sometime in early/mid-2016, Iran will be unshackled from the preponderance of the sanctions regime that halved its oil exports, crashed the value of its currency, and cost the country tens of billions — at least — in lost revenues and additional costs over the course of the past five years. The United Nations Security Council measures, which served as a platform for most of the actions undertaken by the rest of the world against Iran, will vanish with a few notable exceptions pertaining to conventional arms and ballistic missiles.

The totality of European Union sanctions, including the embargo on Iranian oil and prohibitions on energy investment, will evaporate. And nearly all of the American measures that had effectively severed Iran's economy from the international financial system will be waived, permitting somewhere in the realm of $100 to $150 billion in Iranian assets that had been held in overseas accounts to flow back into Iran.

The agreement also provides for the effective cessation of a number of American measures that were predicated on the full range of concerns about Iranian policies, re-opens a loophole that permits U.S. corporations to trade with or operate in Iran via foreign subsidiaries, and carves out a wider array of permissible U.S. business with Iran than at any time since the comprehensive embargo was put in place twenty years ago. Like the release of Iran's frozen assets, these new openings in the American sanctions architecture will go into effect immediately after Tehran's initial nuclear constraints have been certified.

This wide-ranging sanctions relief incorporated in the JCPOA has elicited considerable angst among some here in Congress, as well as other U.S. policymakers and allies. The sense of affront at the appearance of rewarding Tehran after decades of bad behavior is magnified by the irony that Washington is being forced to cede the most effective instrument in its policy toolbox, at the very moment when its efficacy has finally been confirmed, even as some of the most strategically relevant aspects of the Iranian challenge remain unabated. That inescapable reality underscores the importance of identifying and implementing new mechanisms for addressing Iran's problematic regional policies.

Sanctions Relief and the Iranian Economy: What Will Tehran Do with the Money?

The public discussion of the JCPOA and its provisions regarding sanctions relief has tended to emphasize the availability of new resources for Tehran's support for terrorist groups and other violent proxies as well as its assiduous efforts to extend its influence across the broader Middle East. However, it should be acknowledged that the most pressing needs facing the Iranian government are not those related to its regional posture, but rather to its domestic economy.

The sanctions regime erected between 2006 and 2015 has been viciously effective, halving Iran's oil exports, precluding Tehran from repatriating its hard-currency profits from the sales, and impeding Iranian banks from transactions with the rest of the world. They succeeded in shifting Iran's approach to the protracted nuclear impasse not because of these restrictions impeded its ability to sustain its regional policies, but rather because of the more immediate and potentially unsettling implications for the stability and ultimately the survival of the regime.

The sanctions were felt far more immediately and far more profoundly by the average Iranian than the average beneficiary of Tehran's terrorist subsidies, and it was the concerns about the long-term erosion of Iran's economic base and the legitimacy of the ruling system that generated a consensus decision among the political elite to relinquish its longstanding nuclear recalcitrance, elevate a more pragmatic elective leadership, and engage in a serious and, eventually, successful process of negotiations to end the impasse and the sanctions.

For this reason, it is important to appreciate that domestic requirements and priorities will indeed loom large in the allocation of the deal-related windfalls that will accrue to Tehran over the course of the next year. Iran's president, Hassan Rouhani, is keenly concerned with Iran's dire economic predicament. He has consistently articulated a national security perspective in which economic strength is an integral component of national power. He was one of the first public critics of the policies of his predecessor, Mahmoud Ahmadinejad, raising alarms about the dangers of the government's blithe disregard of the implications of intensifying sanctions and the 2008 global financial crisis.

His campaign for the presidency was grounded in the argument that Ahmadinejad's policies had devastated Iran's economy, and after taking office Rouhani has insisted that the situation was even worse than he previously understood. On his 100th day in office, he gave an address to the nation in which he described food shortages, epic inflation rates of 46 percent, and massive state debts of at least 2 trillion rials. He conceded that "the government that had the most revenues during its two terms" – Ahmadinejad presided over eight years in which Tehran earned more in petroleum exports than the previous century of production – "left the most debts as well."

In practice, economic rehabilitation has ranked at the top of Rouhani's agenda, in parallel with the nuclear file. He has installed an experienced group of technocrats and experienced economic planners to manage Iran's rehabilitation, most of who had been forced out of government by Ahmadinejad. They have sought to revive the economy without imposing strict austerity budgeting, imposing fiscal and monetary discipline to control and reduce inflation while attempting to avoid triggering a deeper recession.

Rouhani's government has also sought to abandon or significantly modify several of the headline economic initiatives of his predecessor, and to cultivate greater transparency and accountability within the economy. His officials and allies have been sharply critical of what they describe as incompetent, corrupt, and ultimately destabilizing stewardship of the country by Ahmadinejad and his cronies. And they have endeavored to curtail or even reverse the array of makeshift mechanisms for coping with sanctions that were intended to mask the dramatic exodus of foreign investors that facilitated the creeping sway of the Revolutionary Guard throughout Iran's economy.

One of Rouhani's most significant, and widely appreciated, domestic accomplishments since taking office in August 2013 is the reduction in the inflation rate, from 42 percent at the time of his inauguration to more recent figures of 15 percent. His policies have also reversed the dangerous involution of Iran's economy that transpired during Ahmadinejad's final years in office – stabilizing to minimal levels of growth after a contraction of more than 8 percent.

But he has promised the Iranian people more than just a halt to the crisis; Rouhani has pledged to generate growth, development, and jobs. He acknowledged in February 2015 that "at the moment we are just paving the way and filling up those potholes that were created earlier... We should reach a stage where the ground is paved, after which the machine [of economic growth] will speed up." And he emphasized, in contradistinction to Iran's supreme leader and some hard-line supporters of the Islamic Republic that "those who think the country can develop without relations with the outside world are absolutely wrong."

The JCPOA and its attendant sanctions relief will greatly facilitate Iran's economic rehabilitation, but Rouhani and his advisers are particularly aware that it will not be a magic bullet. Based on their experience during the early 1990s, when a moderate Iranian president sought to reconstruct Iran's economy after a decade of revolution and war, Iranian technocrats appreciate all too well that even the expeditious lifting of all international sanctions will only create new dilemmas for the country's economy.

For this reason, one of the key aspects of Rouhani's economic strategy is an attempt to avoid some of the pitfalls that undermined its previous attempt to rebuild and restore its economy. Then, initial economic improvements were undercut by rapid growth in imports, which contributed to inflation as well as government struggles to stay current on a quickly-expanding foreign debt burden. The potentially counterproductive ramifications of a massive injection of new capital explains in part the conservative estimations by Iran's Central Bank of the prospective repatriation of frozen funds in the aftermath of sanctions relief.

Rouhani and his team will instead seek to deploy the JCPOA economic boost toward job creation and sustainable growth. Masoud Nili, Rouhani's senior economic advisor who has long experience in devising Iran's economic plans, has warned that if Tehran does not invest in its own capabilities and citizens, "in view of the unemployment situation we have, conditions in the economy will become deadly."

As with all issues in Iran, Rouhani's economic policies have generated fierce debate within the engaged political class within the Islamic Republic. However, like the nuclear diplomacy, the president clearly benefits from the support of Iran's supreme leader and, by extension its hard-liners, to advance this agenda.

This isn't simply a matter of policy preferences for Rouhani and his team: Iran has real politics, including elections for its parliament and the body that selects its supreme leader early next year. And its population is impatient to reap the peace dividend that they were promised more than two years ago, when they elected Rouhani to the presidency by a surprising margin. Rouhani's initial stabilization efforts have been greeted positively, but the wait for real results has proven to be a long and frustrating one for Iranians.

The November 2013 interim nuclear agreement sparked new interest in Iran, but it generated little new investment and only modest new avenues of trade for Tehran. To date, the nuclear diplomacy has provided no meaningful 'trickle-down' effect for Iran's economy or its population at large. Expectations have been elevated by the maximalist rhetoric that Iranian leaders have utilized in describing the benefits of the JCPOA.

For this reason, expectations for Implementation Day are sky-high at home among Iranians, and Rouhani will be risking his mandate and his presidency if he does not deliver on real results: the generation of jobs, growth, new vitality and opportunities for Iranians beyond the inner circle of regime elites, whose proximity to power has enabled them to thrive under even the most stringent periods of international economic pressure. (Of course, the *aghazadeh* and crony capitalists of the Islamic Republic are at least as eager for their own piece of the sanctions-relief pie, and the competition for resources among privileged constituencies and state institutions will also place domestic pressure on the regime.)

These priorities do not negate the legitimate concerns about the potential for additional regional troublemaking as a result of the inevitable boost to Iran's economy that will derive from the deal. Rouhani is not Iran's ultimate authority, and the influx of previously inaccessible revenues will magnify the challenge facing the U.S. and the international community with respect to Iran's regional influence.

Still, both the contemporary balance of power in Iran and the historical track record highlight the importance of domestic priorities for Tehran. The internal expectations and urgent demands on the regime's expanding coffers is a more complicated environment than simply a blank check to terrorist groups, and the continuing U.S. capacity to isolate those entities and individuals within Iran who remain engaged in terrorist activities will be crucial to shaping the decisions of its leadership (and the trajectory of its economic recovery.)

How Will Sanctions Relief Impact Iran's Regional Policies?

Unfortunately, the long-term track record is clear: Iran's support for terrorism has never been driven primarily or even substantially by resource availability. In fact, Iran's most destructive regional policies have been undertaken and sustained even at times of epic constraints. These policies were initiated in the early post-revolutionary period, when Iran's economy was suffering the consequences of revolutionary upheaval and continuing internal unrest, and they continued and actually significantly intensified after the September 1980 Iraqi invasion of Iran and throughout the long, brutal, and costly war that followed. In fact, many of Iran's worst regional abuses took place during this first decade: the cultivation of Hezbollah and that group's 1983 bombing of the U.S. Marine barracks in Beirut and the direct and often deadly assistance to subversive groups in its southern Gulf neighbors throughout the war with Iraq. In fact, economic constraints may have energized and legitimized Tehran's investment in unconventional warfare against its neighbors as well as American interests and allies by virtue of the limitations on Tehran's ability to resupply its conventional war effort vis-à-vis Iraq and the cultivation of its leadership's innate sense of suspicion.

These same trends have held over the course of the past decade, as externally-imposed economic pressures on Tehran, as a result of both sanctions and the more recent decline in oil prices, reached or even surpassed the heights of the hardships during the war. These pressures provided no remedy to Iran's efforts to extend its influence through nefarious activities and allies, or its substantial investment in fueling and fighting conflicts in Iraq and Syria. Even since 2010, when the world has applied unprecedented financial pressure on the regime including measures that have directly targeted the institutions and assets related to Iran's regional power projection and its support for terrorist proxies beyond its borders, there is little evidence that sanctions impeded Iran's most destabilizing policies.

The relative consistency of Iran's relationships with terrorist organizations and extremists across the region makes it impossible to discern much, if any, remedial relationship between the economy and the adoption of more responsible regional policies. This is in part a function of the relatively low funding threshold for these activities; the expense associated with sustaining Hezbollah's massive rocket arsenal or fueling Bashar Al Assad's barrel bombs is relatively easily absorbed even at times of relative scarcity. More importantly, the persistence of these policies is further confirmation that they tend to reflect opportunism on the part of Iranian leaders rather than budget priorities.

The few episodes in which Iran's support for terrorism has been mitigated, if only partially and ultimately temporarily, have been undertaken when the risks appear to be too high. During the late 1990s, Tehran appeared to curtail its previous policies of assassinating dissidents abroad as well as reign in its longstanding support to some subversive elements in the Gulf states; these shifts transpired after the 1996 Khobar Towers bombing and the 1997 Mykonos verdict, both of which posed brief but very serious jeopardy to Tehran's efforts to secure a durable rapprochement with its neighbors, reopen its economy to the world, and attract a steady flow of new foreign investment.

What is also plainly evident is that there is a powerful correlation between the intensification of multilateral sanctions on Iran and the expansion of the political and economic influence of the Revolutionary Guards within the power structure of the Islamic Republic. Indeed, during the same years that the Iranian nuclear impasse intensified, and economic pressure mounted, the political and economic role of the Revolutionary Guards expanded markedly.

The Guards' ascendance had been long in the making, and it certainly reflects other factors well beyond sanctions themselves, including the coming-of-age of Iran's war generation and the inability of the reformist movement to sustain its initial momentum and efficacy. Still, it can be no coincidence that the IRGC and its affiliated organizations managed to secure new primacy after sanctions and concerns about political and reputational risks had sent most of Iran's Western investors running.

The Role of Residual Sanctions in Shaping Iran's Regional Posture

The deal leaves intact a significant array of restrictions for Iran's economy. The U.S. Treasury Department remains the long pole in the international sanctions architecture, and even residual American measures will pose a powerful deterrent against business in Iran. Iran's worst actors, including those associated with the Revolutionary Guard Corps, will remain sanctioned by the United States — tainting, by extension, any foreign company that does business with them after the deal.

For American firms and individuals, the embargo on U.S. trade and investment in Iran criminalizes even the most tangential involvement in the Iranian economy outside the specific sectors exempted under the deal.

These measures will compound other complications for new and returning investors in Iran. A decade of increasingly wide-ranging restrictions and consistently rigorous enforcement, including numerous multimillion dollar penalties, has created a culture of compliance by major firms around the world. In fact, the legal and reputational risks have been so thoroughly reinforced that the impact of the openings provided to Iran's economy under the November 2013 interim agreement has proven to be less, not more, valuable than originally anticipated. The same could prove true with respect to the relevant provisions of the JCPOA.

Congressional opposition to sanctions termination means that the Obama administration will have to rely on waivers and other inherently temporary mechanisms for reversing existing measures; that alone entails sufficient uncertainty to give major investors around the world significant qualms about committing to the kind of multi-year, multi-billion dollar projects that Iran's energy sector requires.

And of course the deal incorporates the threat of "snapping back" other sanctions, something the Obama administration fought for and has trumpeted in its defense of the agreement. Even if these provisions are not perfect guarantees that the current level of multilateral restrictions on Iran can be readily reinstated, they reinforce a sense of uncertainty about the medium or long-term context for investing in Iran – a time horizon that will be directly relevant for the scale and duration of major investments.

There is no doubt that the perpetuation of economic restrictions will have a continuing, albeit modest, dissuasive impact on Iran. It seems highly unlikely, however, that U.S. penalties against the Revolutionary Guards and related organizations can provide sufficient disincentives to alter Tehran's longstanding patterns of regional power projection or revise the broad calculus of opportunism and insecurity that underlies these policies and relationships.

Where U.S. sanctions may play the most constructive role is in diminishing the advantages that the Guard and its affiliates have enjoyed within Iran's economy.

Sanctions Worked, So Why Are We Ceding Our Most Effective Tool?

Three decades of indifference to American penalties had inculcated an illusion of invulnerability among the Iranian leadership. With the help of Congress and the world, Washington has tested and ultimately shattered that illusion. Authorities put in place in the aftermath of the 9/11 attacks to curtail terrorist financing provided a platform for assembling an unprecedented campaign that access to the international financial system to individual Iranian banks and eventually most of its economy. Changes in energy markets made it possible for the first time to target Iran's oil production without blowback to the global economy or domestic price at the pump. And Iran's internal regression – its conveniently cartoonish then-president Mahmoud Ahmadinejad and the suppression of 2009 pro-democracy protests – facilitated newfound and profoundly valuable cooperation from Europe and much of the rest of the world.

Analysts have often argued that Iranian policies are shaped by varying degrees of pragmatism and a rational assessment of the costs and benefits of its options. On the nuclear program, however, Tehran's uncompromising stance over a dozen years fueled the perception that its leadership would pay any price for the program. That is disproved by this deal. The sanctions instituted over the course of the past five years forced Iran to alter its uncompromising approach.

Iran's president has acknowledged as much. Rouhani has consistently cited the economy in his criticism of the foreign policies of his predecessor, Mahmoud Ahmadinejad, as well as in his public case for the nuclear negotiations, arguing in May 2015 that "the lives, the economy, the market, the money, the value of the national currency of the people depend on the nuclear negotiations."

So, after 36 years, pressure worked, imperfectly and incompletely perhaps, but it worked nonetheless. And now, just as one aspect of the Iranian challenge appears to have been mitigated, the deal relinquishes the very tool that made that success possible despite the fact that Iran's destabilizing regional policies persist.

The fundamental impediment is this: the United States does not have, nor is it likely we could instigate, anything close to the level of multilateral consensus surrounding Iran's regional policies that was built, slowly and through the fortuitous confluence of facilitating circumstances, on the nuclear issue.

Russia clearly does not share our interests in ending the Syrian conflict through the removal of the vicious Assad government; Beijing will not readily jeopardize its energy security to punish Iran for its financial and material assistance to Hamas or Palestine Islamic Jihad. And even our European allies have traditionally exhibited ambivalence on Iranian support to groups such as Hezbollah.

The most recent period of Iran sanctions has been the exception to the rule of the past 36 years; throughout most of the history of the Islamic Republic, Washington found little support even among its closest allies for the application of any economic pressure toward Tehran whatsoever. Some of the conditions that facilitated the more recent consensus, such as historic shifts in the global energy market, remain true today. However, Iran has effectively dispelled some of the other factors, such as the international abhorrence toward its former president, Mahmoud

Ahmadinejad, and the outrage generated over his contested 2009 reelection and the repression of the protests that followed in its wake.

Rouhani's election launched Iran's rebranding, and this alone had begun to undermine cohesion on the strategy toward Tehran. Ultimately, the nuclear agreement will accelerate a process of reintegration into the global economy that likely would have gained momentum even without a resolution to this crisis.

Washington could have sought to thwart this process until or unless Tehran had fully transformed itself into a responsible actor at home and in the region. The uniquely dominant U.S. role in the international financial system affords formidable leverage, and refusing to dismantle the blockade on Iranian banks would have curbed at least some of the world's sudden enthusiasm for opportunities in Iran. Such a scenario may yet transpire, if Congress can muster a veto-proof majority to reject the nuclear deal.

However, the history of U.S. policy since the Islamic Revolution offers little reason to be sanguine about a go-it-alone approach on Iran. Trying to sustain Iran's economic isolation without the participation, or at least the acquiescence, of the rest of the world's major powers would inevitably pose fewer costs for Tehran and greater expenses for Washington in terms of transatlantic relations and American influence around the world. And, based on the track record of the nuclear negotiations since 2002, it almost surely would generate an even less favorable resolution to Iran's nuclear ambitions.

What Can Washington Do?

Sanctions relief under the JCPOA will undoubtedly complicate and likely exacerbate the challenges posed by Iran across the Middle East. However, the nuclear deal mitigates, in a meaningful fashion and for a reasonable duration, one of the most urgent aspects of the Iranian threat, and should facilitate a new and more serious effort to generate a similar multilateral effort to curtail Iranian terrorist financing and materiel support. There are a number of steps that Washington can and should consider:

1) Clarify in advance with our allies how we will respond to a range of potential issues with implementing the deal, including but not limited to clear-cut Iranian noncompliance with its obligations under the deal. This should include a robust European endorsement of the notion of reinstatement of European Union and individual state sanctions adopted after the 2010 United Nations Security Council Resolution 1929.

2) Make certain through both private and public communications that Tehran appreciates the inevitability of continuing enforcement of those residual American sanctions related to counterterrorism, in an effort to preclude or undercut likely Iranian impulse to use this enforcement as a pretext for any failure to adhere to its own obligations.

3) Intensify efforts to enforce existing Security Council prohibitions on the transfer of conventional weapons and ballistic missile technology to Iran, step up efforts to interdict illicit shipments to and from Iran. In addition, the United States should seek to generate new cooperation with Europe and U.S. regional allies on preventing Iranian arming and financing of proxy groups in the region and around the world.

Ms. ROS-LEHTINEN. Thank you very much.

And we have just been called to the House floor for a series of votes, but we will not be able to come back. I will turn in my questions to you. If I can give you a homework assignment, to answer these for me, I would appreciate it.

And let me turn to Mr. Cicilline in the remaining time for the questions. He is recognized.

Mr. CICILLINE. Thank you, Madam Chair.

And thank you again to our witnesses.

I am interested, Dr. Maloney, you said that Iran's support for terrorism has never been determined by availability of resources, which suggests that the advent of additional resources—I guess, explain, sort of, what you mean by that before I——

Ms. MALONEY. I think simply if you look at the long-term track record of the Iranian regime has done around the region, it has not been dictated by either the availability of or the lack of availability of funds. And, in fact, we have seen the intensification of its worst policies, whether it is in Lebanon, Iraq, or in Syria, at times of greatest economic pressure. The regime always finds ways to fund the guns; it is the butter at home that suffers.

Mr. CICILLINE. And certainly the argument has been made that there will be some pressure on Rouhani and the regime to respond to some of the very pressing domestic issues that face the Iranian people. But I would ask each of the witnesses, what are the things—you know, presuming some portion of the sanctions relief will be directed to activities that Iran is currently engaged in in the region, destabilizing activities, and presumably some increase in that, what are the best things that we can do, that Congress can do, to help mitigate the impact of those activities, reduce the likelihood that they will happen, or impose significant costs on Iran for engaging in that activity? What would you recommend as the one or two things, actions we can take as a Congress to respond to that?

I guess start from left to right.

Mr. OTTOLENGHI. Thank you, sir.

I would suggest three things.

The first is that you retain, both Congress retains and the administration retains, legal instruments to go after entities involved in aiding and supporting terrorism. And these instruments also allow you to prod and press allies who in this current climate may be less inclined to take action.

One clear example is the case of the Iranian private airline Mahan Air. Mahan Air has been an accessory to Assad's war crimes by transporting weapons and personnel, including foreign militias, back and forth from Iran to Syria. It continues to do so, as far as my record tells me. The latest flight happened 2 days ago. So they are not deterred.

Now, the problem with Mahan Air is that is only under U.S. sanctions. Europeans have never sanctioned Mahan Air, and, in the current climate, Mahan Air is actually expanding its destinations in Europe. So——

Mr. CICILLINE. I want to give the other witnesses—but you said you had three things. If you could just tick them off.

Mr. OTTOLENGHI. Yes.

The second thing is that a lot of the funds that will go to economic projects in Iran will actually be allocated through public contracts and vendors to IRGC companies. So this will be an indirect way to help IRGC companies get funds.

And the third thing is that a lot of the IRGC personnel has never been sanctioned, will not be affected by travel bans, so will be a lot more free to travel around the world in procurement efforts. Again, going after these individuals more vigorously will help contain their activities.

Mr. CICILLINE. Thank you.

Dr. Levitt?

Mr. LEVITT. Thank you.

In brief, I would just say I completely agree with Dr. Maloney that Iran has funneled money, whether it had it or not, to these types of activities. But it is true that when they have had more money they have funneled more. As I noted, they have cut back on Hezbollah's budget, and we expect that to pop up again.

The general theme here is that there has to be a cost. We have never incurred serious costs, political costs, for actual acts of terrorism—not after the Marine barracks, not after the Embassy, not after Khobar. It would be very interesting to see what happens after we get more information out of Mughassil to see what happens then.

There is a tremendous amount of work to be done, as Emanuel suggested, with the Europeans—formally, in terms of helping them understand the structure, how serious we are about this, and then informally.

And Treasury Department swears up and down, and I believe them, that they intend to go on new dog-and-pony shows of the kind that I went out on when I was the DAS for intel to educate people about the risks of doing business with Iran. We can no longer tell people, "Don't do business with Iran," but we sure can highlight the risks. And the risks are massive, because the IRGC is more embedded in the Iranian economy now than it ever was before. And this would be very effective.

Mr. CICILLINE. Dr. Maloney, I think I have a few seconds left.

Ms. MALONEY. Very quickly, the focus, as Matt has just said, on building a real coalition with Europe, I think, is the kind of kryptonite that we need to go after Iran on these issues. We have spent 36 years trying to find a way to impede Iran's support for terrorism. What worked on the nuclear issue was that kind of international multilateral coalition.

Mr. CICILLINE. Thank you.

I thank the chairman.

Ms. ROS-LEHTINEN. Thank you so much.

And I will just make a last statement before we go vote. The administration has attempted to assuage concerns that Iran will not use its sanctions relief to support terror, that the money is already tied up in other ventures. But, as we have heard, the IRGC is one of the major actors of the Iranian economy, with a presence in nearly every sector.

Administration officials also tell us that U.S. sanctions against IRGC and its officials will not be lifted. However, it is clear that we have only scratched the surface when it comes to sanctioning

IRGC companies. As you pointed out, all of the subsidiaries—and their subsidiaries are not under sanctions like their parent companies. And so how effective can our remaining sanctions be if these subsidiaries remain free from sanctions?

So we will leave that intriguing topic for the next hearing. Thank you so much, ladies and gentlemen.

And, with that, our subcommittee is adjourned.

[Whereupon, at 2:45 p.m., the subcommittee was adjourned.]

APPENDIX

MATERIAL SUBMITTED FOR THE RECORD

SUBCOMMITTEE HEARING NOTICE
COMMITTEE ON FOREIGN AFFAIRS
U.S. HOUSE OF REPRESENTATIVES
WASHINGTON, DC 20515-6128

Subcommittee on the Middle East and North Africa
Ileana Ros-Lehtinen (R-FL), Chairman

September 10, 2015

TO: MEMBERS OF THE COMMITTEE ON FOREIGN AFFAIRS

You are respectfully requested to attend an OPEN hearing of the Committee on Foreign Affairs, to be held by the Subcommittee on the Middle East and North Africa in Room 2172 of the Rayburn House Office Building (and available live on the Committee website at http://www.ForeignAffairs.house.gov):

DATE: Thursday, September 17, 2015

TIME: 2:00 p.m.

SUBJECT: Major Beneficiaries of the Iran Deal: IRGC and Hezbollah

WITNESSES: Emanuele Ottolenghi, Ph.D.
                   Senior Fellow
                   Foundation for Defense of Democracies

                   Matthew Levitt, Ph.D.
                   Fromer-Wexler Fellow
                   Director
                   Stein Program on Counterterrorism and Intelligence
                   Washington Institute for Near East Policy

                   Suzanne Maloney, Ph.D.
                   Interim Deputy Director
                   Center for Middle East Policy
                   The Brookings Institution

By Direction of the Chairman

COMMITTEE ON FOREIGN AFFAIRS

MINUTES OF SUBCOMMITTEE ON _____ *Middle East and North Africa* _____ HEARING

Day___*Thursday*___Date_____*9/17/15*_____Room_____*2172*_____

Starting Time ___*2:07 p.m.*___ Ending Time ___*2:45 p.m.*___

Recesses | *0* | (____to ____) (____to ____) (____to ____) (____to ____) (____to ____) (____to ____)

Presiding Member(s)

Chairman Ros-Lehtinen

Check all of the following that apply:

Open Session ☑   Electronically Recorded (taped) ☑
Executive (closed) Session ☑   Stenographic Record ☑
Televised ☑

TITLE OF HEARING:

Major Beneficiaries Of The Iran Deal: IRGC and Hezbollah

SUBCOMMITTEE MEMBERS PRESENT:

Chairman Ros-Lehtinen; Reps Chabot, Clawson, Deutch, Cicilline, Meng, and Frankel.

NON-SUBCOMMITTEE MEMBERS PRESENT: *(Mark with an * if they are not members of full committee.)*

N/A

HEARING WITNESSES: Same as meeting notice attached? Yes ☑ No ☐
(If "no", please list below and include title, agency, department, or organization.)

STATEMENTS FOR THE RECORD: *(List any statements submitted for the record.)*

SFR - Rep. Connolly

TIME SCHEDULED TO RECONVENE _____
or
TIME ADJOURNED ___*2:45 p.m.*___

Subcommittee Staff Director

Statement for the Record
Submitted by Mr. Connolly of Virginia

The Joint Comprehensive Plan of Action (JCPOA) is an arms control agreement negotiated with Iran, an adversary of the U.S. with an illicit nuclear program and a long record of gross human rights abuses, regional subversion, and support for international terrorism. Until recently, the Iranian regime had no stated intention to curb any of these condemnable activities.

However, the P5+1 negotiations took direct aim at the Iranian nuclear program and scored a historic diplomatic victory by securing verifiable restrictions on the Iranian nuclear program and denying Iran a path to a nuclear weapon.

Supporters of the agreement are under no illusions that the deal is a comprehensive resolution of the myriad issues the U.S. and our allies have with the repressive regime in Tehran and its reprehensible support for terrorist insurgencies in the region. Support for the deal is derived from the fact that it is a viable alternative to war that takes the Iranian nuclear issue off of the table and secures permanent commitments from Iran regarding the peaceful nature of its nuclear program. In other words, it is the diplomatic alternative we sought to attain when we entered into nuclear negotiations.

Supporters of the deal also understand that the U.S. and our allies are battling on many fronts with the Islamic Republic of Iran, a state sponsor of terror. Progress on the nuclear front does not preclude aggressive action to counter Iran's objectionable behavior elsewhere. If anything, it should invigorate and focus our attention on illicit activity carried out by Iran-supported entities such as the Islamic Revolutionary Guard Corps (IRGC), the IRGC's Qods Force, and Hezbollah.

The IRGC has long-been Iran's tool for suppressing dissent at home and sowing instability abroad. The IRGC targets dissidents for incarceration, and the Basij Resistance Force, the volunteer force it commands, helped stamp out a popular uprising in 2009 and 2010. The Qods Force is active in Syria supporting the Assad regime, and the head of the Qods Force, Qasem Soleimani, has recently taken a prominent role in Iraq where the organization previously supported Shiite militias in their attacks on U.S. troops. Hezbollah, like the IRGC and IRGC-QF, continues to act in contravention with several U.N. Security Council Resolutions that authorize sanctions against individuals and entities party to its illicit activities.

The JCPOA will require the U.N to relax nuclear-related sanctions against the IRGC and IRGC-QF once Iran has fulfilled certain commitments that trigger the implementation of the deal. It is important to note that the U.S. can at any time unilaterally snapback U.N. sanctions if we feel that Iran is not in compliance with the JCPOA. Additionally, the U.S. and the U.N. will keep in place sanctions related to weapons proliferation, human rights abuses, efforts to suppress freedom of expression in Iran, and support for international terrorism. In fact, no U.S. sanctions on the IRGC will be lifted under the JCPOA. Congressionally mandated sanctions contained in the Iran Threat Reduction and Syria Human Rights Act (ITRSHRA, P.L.112- 158) and the Comprehensive Iran Sanctions, Accountability, and Divestment Act (CISADA, P.L. 111-195) will continue to target IRGC finances.

The enumeration of the significant restrictions on Iran under the JCPOA is not to say that our job is done – quite the opposite actually. It highlights the opportunity Congress and the Administration have to work together on expanding our efforts to counter Iranian subversion. The JCPOA does not preclude this collaboration, and the President has written to Congress reiterating his intention to "ensure Israel's Qualitative Military Edge" and strengthen regional partnerships able to deal with Iran's destabilizing activities and support for terrorism.

The President will receive the authority required to waive limited Iranian sanctions and adhere to the commitments made in the JCPOA. What we need now is for opponents of the deal to acknowledge that reality and work in a constructive manner to address the other areas where Iran's actions put it in direct conflict with the security interests of the U.S. and our allies.